To think of the disabled brings thoughts of lost possibilities, but all are "fearfully and wonderfully made" to serve and glorify the Lord. To be found in *Billy & Dave* is the wonder of God's infinite love and his omniscient calling of two brothers with challenges to be a blessing not only to their remarkable family, but to all who learn their story. "To God be the Glory."

Martha T. Bultman
Author of the original Friendship Series
Member of the Reformed Church in America Task Force on Disabilities

What a tender story this little book tells! Have you have ever wondered out loud—or down in the recesses of your heart—if nothing can separate you from the love of God? Nothing? Truly? The story of Billy and Dave will strengthen you. If you haven't wondered, it will make you wiser. It shouldn't take long to read, unless, as I did, you have to stop periodically to weep and pray, "I believe, help my unbelief." Read this testimony of God's faithfulness, and his promise that "those who sow in tears will reap with songs of joy" will be more vivid and compelling than you have ever known.

Ben Patterson
Campus Pastor, Westmont College

This book portrays Dave as he was and the process of his struggle, growth, and courage. The highlight of how God used all members of this family to undo the damage of those early years is most remarkable.

Truman G. Esau, M.D.
former Medical Director of Old Orchard Hospital

Steadfastness. Steady under pressure—an incredible gift of the Spirit found in a family where faith is a way of life. Courage and discouragement, trust and disbelief thread through this story of deep pain and surprising joy. No phony God-talk here! In the journey through their broken world they draw on the grace of the Lord Jesus Christ and the ultimate goodness of their heavenly Father. Their honesty in sharing is like a light "set on a hill," showing all of us the way.

Gladys Hunt
Writer, lecturer, and conference speaker

Bill and Helen Brownson have written one of the most inspiring family stories I have read of the transforming power of love and faith. The emotions of your heart and soul will overflow as you feel the Brownsons' passionate love of Billy and Dave. I am inspired by the devotion of Bill and Helen as parents to be faithful, patient, unconditional, available, and persevering with Billy and Dave as they matured into their potential as children of God. There are so many wonderful lessons I absorbed from Billy and Dave. Most significantly for me, their lives illuminated the authenticity that as a Christian I need to care more for others. This book is a must read over and over again.

Glenn Van Wieren
Men's Basketball Coach, Hope College

Billy & Dave

From Brokenness to Blessedness

With much love,

Bill & Helen

Billy & Dave

From Brokenness to Blessedness

BILL AND HELEN BROWNSON

Words of HOPE

Published in the United States by Credo House Publishers,
a division of Credo Communications, LLC, Grand Rapids, Michigan.
www.credocommunications.net

Published in partnership with Words of Hope.

Words of Hope's mission is to proclaim Jesus Christ through broadcasting in the languages of the world's peoples, seeking with our partners in ministry to build the church by winning the uncommitted to faith in Christ and by encouraging Christians in the life of discipleship.

To respond to the message of this book, for more information about the ministry, and for details on how to order additional copies of *Billy & Dave*, please contact us at

Words of Hope
700 Ball Ave. NE
Grand Rapids, MI 49503-1308

Email: woh@woh.org
World Wide Web: www.woh.org

ISBN: 978-0-9787620-0-1

Cover design by *Karl Rouwhorst*
Interior design and composition by *Sharon VanLoozenoord*

Printed in the United States of America

10 9 8 7 6 5 4 3 2 1

First Edition

We dedicate this book
to Jim and Jonathan, our two
remaining sons, who have lived
with us the story of Billy and Dave,
and who also vastly cheer
our hearts amid grief and loss.

Acknowledgements

We could never have brought this book-dream to fulfillment without Sue Van Otteren of Words of Hope. Her skills in word processing, her prompt attention to every detail in the project, and her evident joy in helping have encouraged us again and again. Thanks so much, Sue!

We deeply appreciate also the work of Liz Murphy, who transcribed with care and skill Dave's sometimes barely decipherable handwriting! You brought the text to light, Liz.

We have been heartened also by those who have carefully read our drafts at various points along the way and have made excellent suggestions, especially Ruth Endean, Dave Bast, and sons Jim and Jonathan. For your time, effort, and heart, we bless you.

For the numerous friends who have told us how much they have longed to read a book about Billy and Dave, and who keep cheering us on, our gratitude knows no bounds.

To all those at Words of Hope who have encouraged us, and made this their witness as well as ours, and to Tim Beals for his kind and helpful editorial work, we express our deep thanks as well.

We feel indebted to all the therapists who gave care and support to Dave during his long struggle. We especially treasure the tireless ministry of Dr. Truman Esau, Dave's psychiatrist and our lifelong friend. Over a span of 25 years, he kept helping Dave and us with his insights and compassion. Thank you, Truman!

This has been truly a labor of love, seeking to tell the tale of our two departed sons, and we have sensed the love and leading of our heavenly Father all along the way. Blessed be your name, O Lord!

Contents

Preface

This is a story about two sons, Billy and Dave, and the family of which they were a part. It is also a story of loss—the different kinds of losses that Billy and Dave each experienced and the things their family lost as a result. In the early 1950s Bill and Helen Brownson were the parents of a young and growing brood. Deeply devoted to one another and to the Lord, committed to serving him in ministry, the Brownsons were the very picture of a happy, active Christian family.

Bill was serving as a pastor in New Jersey while completing his Doctor of Theology degree at Princeton Seminary. Helen shared with Bill in ministry to congregation and community, while keeping their home and welcoming a succession of beautiful baby boys into the household. Then tragedy struck in the form of a life-threatening illness to Billy, the Brownson's oldest child. For days Billy's life hung in the balance, until finally the crisis passed and all the desperate prayers for healing were answered. But gradually it emerged that though his life was spared, Billy's severe illness had not left him unscathed. He was not the same bright, energetic little boy he had been. Eventually the Brownsons would be faced with the realization that their first-born son would never be the same again, and that their hopes and expectations for him would be forever altered.

The Brownsons lost Billy when he was 24. Though the life he lived with his impairment was not the one his loved ones would necessarily have chosen for him, Billy's life was nevertheless rich and happy; and he died full of grace, and deeply loved.

But this was only the beginning of sorrows for the Brownson family. Not long after Billy's death Dave, the second son in the family, began to struggle with depression and feelings of deep anxiety. He soon spiraled downward into severe mental illness, an illness from which he never fully recovered. To the loss of Billy were added these deeper and even more painful losses—of Dave's health and wholeness, at times his sanity, and his hopes and dreams of a career and family of his own.

This is the brokenness of which the Brownsons' title speaks. It was real, and long-lasting. There were no quick fixes, no miracle answers to agonized, often-repeated prayers for healing. But the blessing they experienced and to which they testify was equally real. When Bill and Helen married they dedicated themselves and any children they might have to one supreme goal, expressed in a phrase from Ephesians 1:12. Their deepest prayer was that their lives would all be lived "for the praise of his glory." Though in ways unexpected and painful, God gave them their heart's desire for their family.

Read this book. It will move you. It will encourage you. It may also change your deepest prayers, both for those you love and for yourself.

—*David Bast*

President and Broadcast Minister, Words of Hope

Foreword

This is the story of two sons, the first and second of four. It's about Billy and the handicaps he suffered from measles encephalitis. It's about Dave and his struggle with acute mental illness. Both died suddenly; Billy at 24 and Dave at 49.

It's a pain-filled story of suffering and loss, two young lives severely injured and deprived.

It's also a beautiful story of blessing out of brokenness, joy springing up in the midst of sorrow. It's the story of a family system hard hit by a double trauma, struggling for decades with the effects of it, yet seeing God's hand at work and finding strong encouragement.

It's our grateful tribute to Billy and Dave, whose courage and grace under pressure still stir us to wonder and admiration.

It's our offering to other families stricken in similar ways.

It's our witness to the love from which no affliction can ever separate us.

It's our story. We hope that you may find it helpful in yours.

—*Bill and Helen Brownson*

Our living family members are sons Jim and Jonathan with their wives, Kathy and Jenny. The grandchildren are six in number: Rachel, Anna, and Will in Jim's family; Ben, Joanna, and Sam in Jonathan's.

1

Billy's Illness

From Bill

"Billy is sick! He's trembling all over and he complained of his head hurting, too. Can you come right away?"

It was Helen's voice, calling from upstate New York. She had gone with our four boys to her parents' home in Ballston Spa. After driving the family there, I had come back to our home in Lodi, New Jersey, where I was directing a Daily Vacation Bible School in our first pastorate. It was Thursday morning, June 25, 1959, the next to last day of our Bible school, and I was looking forward to Friday noon when I could leave to join my family again. Then this numbing news, and suddenly I was headed north for the three-hour drive sooner than I had expected.

I felt a gnawing pang of guilt. In my preoccupation with the details of Bible school, I hadn't even thought of Billy's needs in my prayers that morning. Billy was almost seven, the oldest of our boys. He had finished first grade and was already reading well above his grade level. For the last few days he hadn't quite seemed himself. Two of the others had been sick with measles, and we thought that perhaps Billy was coming down with it, too. But he hadn't broken out yet. He had complained of pain in his head. We remembered one night when he woke up screaming, clutching his head in his hands as though trying to hold it together. And on the trip up the New York Thruway, he had seemed unusually irritable. I recalled how I had felt a vague uneasiness about his condition then.

But our mood that day as we made the trip together had been for the most part a happy one. Helen and I had reminisced about many of the golden moments we had shared. The goodness of God to us had seemed especially vivid and real. I actually said something like this: "Even if the rest of our lives were difficult and filled with suffering, we would still have had more than our share of happiness."

Those words were coming back to me now as I sped through mile after mile of New York woodland. I wondered about Billy, and as I wondered I prayed. Just how sick was he? Surely it wasn't too serious. As the trip wore on I found it hard to concentrate, hard to keep in mind what had happened. I thought of how I had been away from Helen for several days and how much I wanted to be with her again. I thought of my recent visit to a church in Chicago that had shown interest in calling me as its pastor. Then with a little twinge of conscience for having forgotten him, my thoughts would turn again to Billy. "Lord, be with him; Lord, heal him . . ."

It was mid-afternoon when I turned into the driveway at the Stewart farm. I was glad to arrive but taut with excitement as I raced into the empty kitchen and up the stairs. Everyone had gathered in the middle bedroom and there Billy was lying, looking very small on that wide bed.

Seeing him shook me. His whole body was trembling. I remember especially the way his lips twitched and his eyelids fluttered. He hardly looked like the bright-eyed little boy I knew. With hardly a word to the others in the room, I said with a kind of half-confidence, "He's going to be all right." I remember putting my hands on his head and praying right then that he would be healed. I seemed to have an assurance that my prayer would be heard, even though the twitching continued and he showed no signs of recognizing me.

Now there was time to greet Helen, Mom and Pop Stewart, and Florence, Helen's twin, who was also visiting at that time. They had been doing all they could to keep Billy's fever down while they waited for a doctor to arrive. It was one of those doctors' afternoons off and finding one who would visit the home had proved quite difficult. Finally, after what seemed a very long time, the doctor came up the steps. He examined Billy, asked a few questions, and then made arrangements for him to be admitted to a hospital in Schenectady. The doctor's mood seemed somber, almost bitter. He knew what this meant far better than we did at the time. And he hated what he saw.

Pop Stewart drove us down to the hospital in his car. I sat in the back seat with Billy, watching intently for some little sign of improvement. It seemed to me that the trembling was less violent. *Maybe he'll come out of it soon,* I thought.

As soon as Billy was brought into a hospital room, the nurses worked rapidly to bring down his fever. They wrapped him in sheets wet with ice water, and changed them frequently. It seemed to work. His temperature began to drop from a high of 108 degrees.

The doctors didn't seem too communicative. They ran several tests on him, checking, I learned, for the possibility of spinal meningitis. About an hour later, the news came. "This is pretty grim. The boy may not live, and if he does survive, his brain may be seriously damaged. I'm afraid I can't give you much hope. I'm sorry."

Billy was resting quietly now and there didn't seem to be any more need for us at the hospital at that time, so Pop and I drove back to the farm. As I got in the front seat of the car, everything let loose inside me. I sobbed and cried most of the way home. I wasn't bitter, at least I didn't feel that way. I was just hurt, hurt more than I'd ever been before. Pop was good for me. He quietly drove and let me cry it out.

I had called Helen with the news before we left the hospital, so when I returned to the farm, we had a chance to be by ourselves and talk about it for the first time since I had come up from New Jersey. I was over the initial shock by then, struggling to prepare for what might lie ahead. Helen had been dealing with her pain as well.

From Helen

My encounter with family sadness had begun when I was a small child. Ours was a busy life on a fruit and dairy farm in upstate New York. When my twin sister and I were scarcely three years old, our only brother was born, named after my father. We were very proud of his middle name, Alexander, for it appeared on all the old cemetery grave stones near our farm—dating back to the Revolutionary War.

Something grievous happened when our brother was three years old. Perhaps there was an accident, and Edward Alexander had suffered brain damage. Or could it have been PKU, a disease that leads to retardation and for which tests were not given at that time? Our doctors couldn't agree on a diagnosis, and we were puzzled. But Eddie couldn't talk. His behavior began to seem bizarre; we couldn't predict what he would do. We began to feel troubled about his actions. We struggled with vague feelings of uneasiness and sadness; we all needed help. The subject was not mentioned often; it seemed to be one of those private family matters you didn't talk about.

But there was embarrassment. I remembered one incident when we children (Florence and I, Janet, Judy, and Eddie) were playing in our backyard. A distinguished gentleman had driven up. He stepped out of his car and headed for our group. He turned to Eddie, my handicapped brother. "Good afternoon, son. I wonder if I could talk to your mother or father." Eddie said nothing. Suddenly I felt ashamed. How could I explain to this impressive looking man that my brother couldn't talk? Finally I gained some courage: "My brother can't talk," I apologized. "My mother is inside the house; I'll get her."

I never forgot those feelings of self-consciousness. That simple encounter filled me with pain as a sister of a handicapped child. I continued to feel that through all my growing-up years. I feared that there would always be a need for explanations.

My mother and father were hard pressed. They wondered what to do since there were no special education classes in the schools then. How could they manage the burden of a child wandering off or showing unpredictable behavior? They couldn't watch him constantly on a busy farm, around other children and hired hands.

On one bitterly cold winter day, we couldn't find Eddie anywhere. A search began. We finally found him half frozen. Something had to be done. I can still remember when the doctor came to our home. We children knew that grim decisions were being made. All of us had a sense of dread.

Soon afterward, the whole family piled into our Plymouth and drove to a state school for retarded children in western New York. The brick-walled facility seemed monstrous to us. There we left an eight-year-old boy, alone on his cot in a ward of over fifty beds. We drove home in tears.

Shortly after this family ordeal, a Daily Vacation Bible School was held in our church, and I first heard the good news of Jesus. My teacher was a teenager who had recently trusted in Christ herself. We small children drank in the message of forgiving grace, eternal life, and Christ's presence with us. We invited him into our lives. Though I was only nine years of age, the experience proved memorable for me. I rushed home and made a poster, which I hung on the wall: "I, Helen Stewart, received Jesus Christ as my Savior at DVBS. My life verse is John 3:16."

I remember feeling then such a concern for my brother. He obviously couldn't understand much of the Gospel's truth, but I wanted so much for him to know God's love as I did. In those days there were no chapel services for residents of institutions to attend. I am afraid my brother seldom heard of spiritual things.

Later, when I was 14 years old, I experienced another time of trouble. I was terrified. I felt as if I had fallen into a long dark tunnel with only a faint glimmer of light far away. Voices seemed distant, people removed from me, and covers heavy on my feet. I thought, "I must be seriously ill." I knew my body ached all over and I could scarcely walk when they took me in an ambulance to the hospital.

I had acute rheumatic fever, and the illness came to dominate my life. Since those were the days before antibiotics, doctors were concerned about whether I would recover. I began to sense a grim foreboding. Would I die? My fears began to grow, and in desperation I cried to the Lord. I wanted to live for him and I didn't want to go to heaven yet.

I remained in bed for six months, a time filled with much soul-searching and personal growth. I discovered the loving unselfishness of my family, along with kindly caring from other friends.

Stresses on our family, slow recovery from rheumatic fever, and struggles to discover my own identity occupied most of my teenage years. One day, however, a man walked into my life who felt as I felt, who loved God, and who wanted to serve him. We could talk easily and pray together. He embodied all that I felt I wanted in a husband. I was overjoyed when Bill Brownson asked me to consider being his life-partner!

We had experienced a growing closeness in our courtship and marriage. Seminary days were rich and full, and graduate school at Princeton proved a growing time as well. God had given us four splendid boys, and we had committed each of them to the Lord as they were born. We had entered into an exciting time at Lodi, New Jersey, in which God richly blessed our ministry. We had good health and daily provisions for our needs. We didn't realize then that this period of "normal living" was providing us with the resources we would need for the many testings that were to come later. Daily blessings called for daily thanksgivings and challenged us to grow deeper in God.

From Bill

As the full impact of Billy's illness began to settle upon us, I said to Helen, "If we're going to lose Billy, we'll just have to accept it." I felt that's what I needed to say. Didn't the Lord pray, "Nevertheless, not my will but thine be done"? I think I was a little shocked at Helen's reply. "Yes, but let's wrestle for him first." The moment she said it, I knew she was right. Hadn't I preached that? Hadn't I taught that the resignation comes after we have truly prayed, not before? Her words gave me new hope. As long as there was any chance left at all, at least we could pray. We could give ourselves to prayer as we had never done in our lives.

We called some of the people in our congregation in Lodi. They arranged a special prayer meeting for Billy, and we learned afterward that the prayers were halting and infrequent until a little girl began to plead that God would make Billy well. Then prayers and tears came freely from almost everyone.

We called other Christian friends whom we knew would pray for Billy. And pray they did. We had phone calls from several different parts of the country, assuring us that we were being upheld. I remember how friends of ours in North Carolina quoted to us these words from John's Gospel: "This sickness is not unto death, but for the glory of God." They told how this conviction had come to them as they had prayed.

That evening I went back to the hospital, having decided to spend the night in Billy's room. For most of the night I prayed, sometimes on my knees, sometimes leaning back in a chair. Now and then I would doze off and then wake up again to pray. It felt good to be able to spread it all before God. It seemed right to keep on asking, even though he knew how I felt. I had often preached about importunate prayer, but I had never been so persistent in my own asking before.

Early in the evening, an old Christian friend came by and stopped in Billy's room. He was the director of a Bible conference and had been a respected leader of ours for years. His concern, his affection, his simple prayers buoyed my spirit. My hopes grew. Who knows what God will do in answer to so many prayers? Maybe this is to be a vivid demonstration of what we've tried so often to preach, that God does wonderful things in response to the prayers of his people.

From Helen

From my perspective, all these happenings could not have come at a more difficult time, and I found myself struggling. First of all, I was not well. Several weeks earlier I had developed a "strep throat," and despite antibiotics, the infection had gone to my heart again, and a case of rheumatic fever had set in. I knew that rest, low stress, and total inactivity were needed for keeping my heart from damage. (That was the doctor's directive then—it might be different now.)

My sister, Janet, was to be married that summer, and my mother had her hands full planning those events. Because of her caring heart, however, she had invited me with our four lively boys to spend the summer on the farm in the hopes that I could secure good rest there and the boys would be entertained with all the activities going on. It seemed a good idea, but we had not counted on this crisis.

While trying not to allow myself undue stress, now I found our son critically ill! It seemed impossible to remain calm under the circumstances. Bill tried to shield me by staying with Billy, but my heart still pounded over this agonizing situation (both literally and figuratively).

Added to my physical disability, the emotional turmoil of dealing with the grim prognosis overwhelmed me. Death or retardation! What a choice! I felt almost hopeless about full recovery, though I wanted to keep praying for a miracle. For me, this prospect of a retarded son brought back all the family pain I felt I had left when I married Bill. First a brother. Now a son. "Why? Why?" What was God trying to say to me in it all?

I could not believe that the active, lovely son of the day before was now unconscious. The hours that followed that day were filled with shattering fears. In the midst of it all a faithful teacher of the Word arrived and lovingly listened to my worst anxieties.

Then she spoke a word I'll never forget: "Remember, Helen, Jesus loves your child more than you! He regards Billy as one of the special ones he called to himself." I felt comforted.

From Bill

The next day was uneventful. I went to the farm and got some rest, while Helen went down and stayed for awhile with Billy. His fever was down now and he seemed to be in a deep sleep. He sometimes moved around in his bed, but we began to notice that it was only his left side that moved. The doctor seemed to be checking all sorts of things, but we couldn't learn much from him. All we knew was that Billy had suffered a severe case of encephalitis. Apparently in rare cases the measles virus attacks the brain. Billy had never actually broken out with the measles. The convulsions and the high fever had seemed to come on him very suddenly.

It was late in the morning on the second day, about 48 hours after he was stricken, that Billy spoke again for the first time. "I want a drink." What a beautiful sound that was! Why, he spoke as though he hadn't realized he'd been so sick! I was thrilled beyond words. "His mind's all right," I thought. "He can still speak." I raced out to call Helen. Our prayers had been answered!

It was evident, though, that there was something wrong with his right side. He could move his right leg slightly, but it seemed as they tapped here and there on his right arm that there was no response at all. When he began to smile, it was a quirky half smile. The right side of his face didn't seem to get in on the act at all. But slowly, in those first few days of recovery, some movement seemed to come back, at first in his leg and then in the grosser movements of his arm. Maybe the right side would be restored after all.

It thrilled us that Billy could still read. Although he had just finished the first grade, he had been reading on almost a fourth-grade level. And he could read as well as ever—or almost as well. We noticed that every now and then he would miss a word or skip a line. And when he wrote the letters of the alphabet, he seemed to have difficulty forming a few of them. But that seemed a minor thing now. He was alive and making progress and we were deeply grateful. We were confident that all the promise of his young life would yet be fulfilled.

2

Billy's Birth and Early Years

From Helen

William Clarence Brownson IV. That name would not have been my first choice for a son, but I agreed with Bill that a first son should carry on this family tradition. And a marvelous tradition it was.

The first William Brownson was William Greene. He had shared many fruits of Christian character with his father, Simeon. Simeon had moved from Connecticut to upstate New York after the Revolutionary War, and there he farmed and raised sixteen children. We had inherited Simeon's diary, written over a period of thirty years in beautiful script, and describing life vividly in the early 1800s. His deep Christian commitment appeared on every page and led us to thank God frequently for our heritage. He sought to instill Christian faith in all his children and to encourage their education. William Greene graduated from Hamilton College and went on to teach in a school at Jamaica, New York. Later he became the principal.

Soon the Civil War began. William Greene tried to enlist and was denied service because of his poor eyes. Undaunted, he went to medical college to secure the skills necessary to become a surgeon in the Union Army, and his wife carried on at the school as principal. After the war he returned to his family and began to practice medicine in New Canaan, Connecticut. There his son, William Clarence, after training in medical school, joined his father in a practice in New Canaan.

The first William Clarence moved to West Asheville, North Carolina, because of fragile health and the hope that the altitude would encourage his lungs. There the second William Clarence was born, William Clarence Jr., Bill's father. He became an engineer and joined a cement company that eventually called him to the home office in New York City.

When Bill was born, it was again a given that he would carry on the family name. He became William Clarence III. Our Billy was William Clarence IV. The Brownson men had been sensitive, intelligent, and gentle people. Billy had seemed to manifest the same qualities. He was all that we could hope for in a son. We were delighted in him.

From Bill

Billy's birth place was Princeton, New Jersey. Helen and I had settled there during the summer of 1952, as I prepared for doctoral studies at Princeton Seminary in the fall. Like most expectant parents, we had prepared ourselves with names for either a boy or girl, but for me that was only a formality. I longed for a son. In fact, I wanted one so badly that while Helen was in the delivery room I began to feel guilty about that. What if God gave us a precious baby girl? Could I rejoice just as greatly? Certainly, I thought, but I really wondered if I could. I went through quite an inner struggle over that. How ungrateful could a man be? I ought to be overjoyed just to have a baby without worrying about whether or not it's a boy. I think I began then to feel that, and to welcome the joy of possibly having a daughter, when the nurse came with her announcement, "It's a boy!" I felt overwhelmed. Now all the pent-up longing for a son could be released. Who can describe how that feels?

The nurses let me see Helen just as she was coming out from under the anesthesia. And they brought the baby in, too. We beamed at each other. We felt right then that we should commit him to the Lord. Our prayer was that Billy (William Clarence Brownson IV) would live "for the praise of His glory."

That verse from Paul's Ephesians letter had played a large role in our life together already. In the months before we were married, it had seemed that God was calling us to be man and wife, not only for our joy but to serve God's purpose. Again and again that verse found its way into our prayers together. Though we knew that it was meant for all God's people, we took it as his special promise to us. We didn't know exactly how, but we believed and prayed that something of God's love and goodness would be revealed in our life together. The thought was such an absorbing one that we had it engraved inside our wedding rings: Eph. 1:12.

That's why our prayer for Billy later had such profound meaning for us. Here, a year after our marriage, was our first child. God had been marvelously good to us. How we wanted his name to be praised in our firstborn!

Billy's birth also meant a great deal to our parents. For both sides of the family he was the first grandchild. It was my mother who made over him the most. At the time of his birth she was already battling with an illness that was to take her life only nine months later. Perhaps she sensed that he was the only grandchild she would ever hold, and she lavished a wealth of affection on him. And so did each of the other grandparents. Those were happy days for all of us.

By the time Helen and Billy came home from the hospital, we were living in North Hall on the Princeton Seminary campus. Among the many blessings that Billy brought with him was the opportunity to live in accommodations for married students with children. We soon wondered, however, whether the building had actually been designed with families in mind. During our first year at Princeton, we lived in one room complete with adjoining mini-bath and shower stall. That shower stall turned out to be the only place where the baby could even be slightly shielded from the clamor of our all-purpose room. Getting his bottle at night also proved to be quite an undertaking, since the kitchen we shared with another couple was one floor down and at the other end of the building. Ever try negotiating a distance like that with your eyes half shut—at four o'clock in the morning?

By the time Dave was born, mid-way through our second year, we were living in slightly more ample quarters. But even then, when our first new piece of furniture, a Simmons hide-a-bed, was opened up, the floor space in our apartment was reduced to the vanishing point. Like many theological students, we were ready to move into a parsonage—almost any parsonage.

During my second year at Princeton we spent each weekend in a church in Lodi, New Jersey. When I had finished the final year of residence, we moved up to Lodi and began to work there on a more permanent basis. I was ordained in the Presbyterian Church U.S.A. and became the "stated supply" of the congregation in Lodi. Now we could move into our first parsonage.

The outside of the home was in fair condition, except for a perilously rickety front porch. Inside, things were slightly better, although we learned later that little if any change had been made there for the past fourteen years. But the house had one redeeming quality that overshadowed all others. It was large. Thus it seemed to us like a mansion. We loved every square foot of it.

We were hardly settled in our new home when our third boy, Jimmy, was born. Soon after his birth one of the local papers carried a story about the new minister and his wife and family, hinting that there was a long-range plan for a full baseball team. I'll have to admit that the idea had entered my mind more than once. Even when Jonny arrived some three years later, having a baby boy seemed as fresh and wonderful as ever.

Four boys—and Billy was the unchallenged leader of the gang. The church and parsonage stood squarely on Main Street, with the public library about ten feet away on the parsonage side and a line of stores on the other side of the driveway from the church. In back of the church and parsonage was a sizeable parking lot. That was the playground where Billy reigned. He was the director of all activities, the creator of all new games, the shrewd driver of hard bargains. We used to smile at the way he governed his small army.

To a proud father's eye, Billy showed promise of athletic prowess, too. He threw with a smooth southpaw motion and was learning to hit a baseball consistently—not far, but with a fluid level swing. Most of all I reveled in the way he could run. I could stand spellbound just watching him sprint across a field or around the church. What a miler he would make someday!

Billy went to kindergarten and first grade at a school in nearby Passaic. Like a number of left-handed children, he had some difficulty learning to write, and for a while would occasionally slip into writing backward—like his name on a prominently displayed piece of art work. On the whole, however, we were encouraged at his progress, particularly in his reading skills. And at anything requiring memorization, he seemed to excel.

During the spring of 1959 he was assigned the role of narrator for the annual children's program before the parent-teacher organization. Billy had four typewritten pages to memorize. We worked on it with him and were surprised at how effortlessly he seemed to pick it up. On the night of the PTA meeting, we sat in the second row. Billy spoke his part flawlessly. To our eyes, at least, he seemed very much in control of the situation, even in prompting one or two of the other children when they seemed a bit confused.

Billy had gifts of leadership; there was no doubt about that. He was a born public speaker. Perhaps some day he would preach the good news of Jesus Christ. That thought made all his budding potential that much more thrilling to me. Less than a month after the PTA meeting he was stricken.

3

Home Again!

From Bill

It soon became clear that Billy's recovery would take a long time. Some motion was returning to his right side and he was receiving extensive therapy each day, but a hospital stay of at least two or three months seemed to lie ahead for him.

After those first few days I returned to my pastoral duties in Lodi while Helen and our other three boys remained at the Stewart farm. Those were difficult days for Helen. Still weakened from rheumatic fever and away from her husband and home, she found it hard to fight off fears about Billy's future. She had difficulty sleeping at night. And since the boys were in the same room with her, every time they stirred she wondered if another might be ill. She fought her fears with prayer and often repeated the words of a hymn until sleep came.

Two hymns came to have particular meaning for her at that time. One was "God Moves in a Mysterious Way His Wonders to Perform." She played it over and over again on the piano, drinking in its message:

> Judge not the Lord by feeble sense,
> but trust him for his grace.

Behind a frowning providence
he hides a smiling face.

The other hymn was a new one we hadn't discovered before: "My God, How Wonderful Thou Art." Here was a hymn of exalted worship and somehow singing it helped both of us to sense God's nearness and to live in hope.

My God, how wonderful Thou art,
Thy majesty how bright!
How beautiful Thy mercy seat
In depths of burning light!

Back in Lodi the members of the congregation were wonderfully kind to me. Every night I ate in a different home and found healing in the love and concern of warm-hearted people. But the nights were long and I had a lot of time by myself. Daily I was praying for Billy's recovery and searching the Scriptures for some word of divine promise, spreading the whole situation before God as earnestly and believingly as I could.

One morning I opened my Greek Testament to the place where I had last read. I began to read that day in Matthew 12:9. It was about the man with the withered hand! The climax of the narrative came at verse 13:

> Then he said to the man, "Stretch out your hand," and the man stretched it out and it was restored whole like the other.

I was so excited I could feel my flesh tingling. Billy's paralyzed hand was the most evident feature of his disability. This passage seemed to speak directly to his condition. On the blank page opposite that verse in my inter-leaved Greek Testament I wrote this:

> Note: On July 4, 1959, after earnest believing prayer for the restoration of Billy's right arm and leg, I turned to the Scriptures, took up my reading at Matthew 12:9. I take Matthew 12:13 as Christ's word for Billy's healing.

I don't really know what I expected to happen, or when. But I remember the sense of ease I had that my prayer had been heard.

Sometime during each week I drove up to Ballston to be with the family and to see Billy. Later on in the summer I had a few weeks of vacation and could stay with the family over weekends as well. Both Helen and I noticed as time went on that Billy had some mannerisms we hadn't seen before.

He was confined to his bed and his wheelchair, but he seemed to be almost bursting with suppressed feeling. All the energy of a crippled six-year-old came out in shrill whistle-like squeals or in popping the inside of his mouth with his little finger (a trick he had learned from me, I must admit, before his illness). From all we could gather, he seemed to be cheerful when we were away from him, but the moment we would appear in his hospital room he would burst into tears. But we knew that his whole system had received a tremendous shock, and these little habits weren't too surprising.

He seemed different in other ways, too. He couldn't seem to sustain a conversation as once he had. He couldn't seem to think or talk about anything that wasn't present before him. At times he seemed to be in a world of fantasy, not really understanding where he was or what had happened. All this, together with vague hints that nurses and doctors would drop from time to time, made us wonder what changes there were to be in his personality. Just what does brain injury do to a boy?

There were some ways, though, in which he was very much the same Billy. He loved baseball and among the many gifts that began to fill up his room during weeks of convalescence, he prized baseball cards the most. Pop brought them to him when I wasn't there, and when I drove up from Lodi I brought a sizable batch along. I wonder if anyone ever had so many baseball cards! By the end of his stay he had shoe boxes full of them and there were few moments when he wasn't fingering or perusing them.

Many of the things he had learned before his illness were still with him. We had done a good bit of singing in our home, and he had learned a number of hymns. His favorite was "Jesus, Lover of My Soul." He often sang it in the course of his wheelchair journey through the hospital hall, to the great interest of some of the patients. One elderly lady seemed especially touched by it. Afflicted with a lingering illness, she was deeply depressed most of the time. Billy's singing made her cry, but it seemed somehow to cheer her up, too. She looked forward each day to his visit to her room. And every day he sang:

> Jesus, lover of my soul, let me to thy bosom fly,
> While the nearer waters roll, while the tempest still is high.
> Hide me, O my Savior, hide, till the storm of life is past;
> Safe into the haven guide; O receive my soul at last.

As the summer wore on, Helen's condition, as well as Billy's, continued to improve. Her family gave tremendous help and support. Her mother and dad understood what Helen was going through. The Stewarts also had struggled with their own son's problems until finally the state institution had seemed the only safe place for him to be.

Dave, at age five and a half, had been deeply disturbed when Billy became ill. In those first days of the illness he had picked up snatches of our conversation—more than we realized he had. I'll never forget the anguish in his face when he blurted out one day, "I don't want Billy to die!" As time went on we could reassure him more and more that he wouldn't die and that in time he would be able to come home. That made Dave and Jim happy and gave them something to look forward to during the long summer. On nice days they would ride down to the hospital with Pop Stewart or with me and help push Billy around in his wheelchair on the grounds of the hospital.

Billy, meanwhile, was involved in a therapy program that seemed endless. But it was proving effective, particularly in restoring use of his right leg. Just before his release from the hospital in early September, he was fitted with a leg brace and began to try to walk on his own. The first steps were awkward and halting, but they were wonderful to behold. He had a brace on his right shoulder and arm also, but recovery there seemed much more slow and uncertain. He could move his right arm at the shoulder in a limited way, but the finer movement of forearm, wrist and fingers had hardly begun to return at all. He still had a long way to go.

As we began to make plans to bring Billy home from the hospital, we received another jolt—this one financial. The type of hospitalization insurance we had would cover only a very small percentage of the hospital costs, chiefly because the illness and the hospitalization had occurred outside of New Jersey. On August 1 of that summer a new medical insurance went into effect, but since Billy's illness was a pre-existent condition at that date, we received no assistance from that quarter either. But with the money we had saved toward the replacement of our old car we were finally able to pay the bill.

By the first week in September, all of us were back in Lodi eagerly looking forward to the day when, after two and a half months of convalescence, Billy would be able to return home.

Homecoming was a banner day. Once again I was driving down the New York Thruway, this time with Billy in the car, headed for home. The miles went by quickly and soon we were nearing Lodi. Billy was getting more and more excited. Finally the big moment arrived and we drove through the iron gates and stopped in the driveway next to the front porch. The whole family was out to greet us. Billy made straight for the house, and, as if to prove he could still do it, climbed up the steps and walked through the front door. The boys looked on with awe, while we cried for sheer joy. He was home again and he could walk!

Dave and Jimmy seemed to assume that everything now would be as it was before. They wanted Billy out in the back of the parking lot with them for a game of baseball. We weren't sure that was such a good idea, but Billy was all for it, and for a boy with his right leg and right arm in braces, he did pretty well. He could throw almost as well as ever, and he hit the ball surprisingly often with his one-handed swing.

But he wasn't interested in playing baseball for very long. He was hyperactive, moving from one thing to the next, as though driven. While in the house, he would switch lights off and on, open and close doors, and handle everything in sight. Loose objects were thrown or kicked, and if small enough, they were thoroughly chewed. The chewing sometimes became a significant problem. He seemed under special compulsion to chew the collars or sleeves of his shirts. Within a month he had scarcely a shirt left with an undamaged collar. Baseball cards and napkins were part of his regular fare, too. We soon found that neither pleadings nor commands could stop this. He wasn't even aware that he was doing it.

Dave and Jimmy were disappointed when Billy didn't prove very friendly. His limitations seemed to frustrate him. Often he vented his feelings by pummeling or kicking his brothers. Sometimes he seemed to derive pleasure from hurting them. That depressed us. We wondered if it was safe to leave him alone with the other boys, especially with little Jonny.

Other things disturbed us, too. He was almost completely unpredictable. He seemed unable to foresee the consequences of what he did and at times would open one of the car doors when the car was in motion. He ate his food with great haste and sometimes had difficulty keeping it down. Thoroughly exhausted at night, he fell asleep earlier than his younger brothers and then woke early in the morning to make sleep impossible for the whole household.

School was not quite the same as before, either. Billy was in the second grade now, and he seemed capable of doing the work, but his hyperactivity caused serious problems in the classroom. His span of attention was painfully brief. He made life difficult for the children around him. His teacher bore with him patiently and tried to help him all she could, but the situation didn't seem to improve. Certain patterns began to emerge in his work at school. Whatever required rote memory or built upon something he already knew was fairly easy for him. But the power to integrate things in his mind, to relate one thing to another, to imagine creatively, seemed to be impaired.

The people in the congregation saw other differences in Billy and his behavior. Whereas before he had been somewhat shy and reserved, now he seemed completely without inhibition. Some tried to encourage us by pointing out how much friendlier he was than he had been before, but we felt uneasy about the sudden change.

For the first few weeks after Billy returned home, we didn't have him attend the Sunday worship services. One Sunday morning, however, he hobbled over from the parsonage to the church and walked into the sanctuary in the middle of the morning worship service. He called out to me loudly from the rear entrance, and I had a difficult time persuading him to go back to the house.

That day after the service I remember asking Helen what had been in the back of my mind for some time. "Do you think his mind is all right?" It was becoming clear to us more and more that Billy really was different. His personality had changed. His ways of relating to people were altered. He could not think or converse as he had done before. It was almost as if the Billy we had known was gone and a new child, a new Billy, had come into our home.

We had another saddening experience when we took Billy to our family doctor back in Lodi. He examined the boy and asked a number of questions. Then he took Billy's right arm in his hands, probing it, trying to open the clenched hand. Then, suddenly, with an expression of frustration and despair, he released the arm. He said nothing. But what I saw in the doctor's eyes that day chilled my heart.

4

New Beginnings in Chicago

From Bill

Early in July of 1959 I had received a call to become pastor of a congregation in Chicago. The invitation came at the end of a chain of circumstances that seemed to point to God's leading. I had first been asked to preach at this church on Christmas Sunday the year before but had declined, feeling I should not be away from my own congregation on such an important occasion.

Once again in April I had been invited to come and conduct the worship services on a given Sunday, but since I had already been out of town considerably during that month I declined again. When the third invitation came in June I felt that I should at least look into the situation.

The church was at that time a large, flourishing congregation on Chicago's sprawling south side. After the morning service on the day I visited there, I felt ill at ease. The church seemed too large, too well established. After six years in a young, struggling congregation in Lodi, I had difficulty seeing myself in this new setting.

But during the evening service a conviction began to grow with me that this was where I was to minister. In fact, after my flight back the following day, I told my sister (who was serving with her husband at that time in Iselin, New Jersey) that I believed the Chicago church would call me and that I further believed I should accept their call.

But all this had been before Billy's illness. Ten days after my visit to Chicago it seemed that everything had changed for us. When the call came in early July, we were puzzled as to how we should respond. Moving at that time seemed impossible, with Helen still convalescing and Billy's future so uncertain. Our first impulse was to decline the call. But the more we considered it, the more we were convinced that God was leading us to Chicago. But how could that be? We surely couldn't go that summer, or even in early fall.

When I gave my answer to the church toward the end of July, I told them that I would be happy to accept their call but that under the circumstances I would be unable to move to Chicago until the first part of November. When the Chicago consistory graciously agreed to this, we were gladdened and relieved. This would give us time—time for Helen and Billy to recover, time to tie ends together of our ministry in Lodi.

By November 2 we were on our way westward. It was a time of autumn splendor and we thoroughly enjoyed the sights of the trip, although in other ways it was a very tiring one. Billy was restless and difficult to manage, and Helen, though much improved, was still not at full strength. What a delight it was to arrive in Chicago and find that our furniture had already been unpacked and even set in place, and that our refrigerator was liberally stocked with food!

The congregation's first acquaintance with Billy came at a reception they had planned for our family. At one point during the program we were to sing something as a family; I don't remember just what. Jonny, of course, was still a baby, so he wasn't expected to participate, but Helen and I and the three older boys stationed ourselves in the large pulpit area facing the congregation. The moment we got up there I had the feeling that the effort was ill advised. Billy didn't sing, nor did he stand quietly. It was all I could do to keep him from trying to climb up on the pulpit. We tried to smile graciously, but we were troubled and embarrassed. Would our congregation understand?

Some did and some didn't. When he was almost uncontrollable during a church service, or when he disturbed a Sunday school class, Billy's behavior would cause some to whisper that "all he needed was some good firm discipline." And sometimes we almost believed that.

In some ways Billy seemed quite normal. For a second-grader he was still remarkably articulate. We wondered: Was he simply spoiled from all the attention he had received? How much of his misbehavior was brain damage and how much could be controlled by discipline? We wrestled with that question for a long time. He had been a well-behaved little boy before his illness. Much of the problem had to be the result of the encephalitis, we concluded.

In his third-grade class Billy seemed capable of doing the work, but he was exceedingly hard to manage. His attention span was distressingly short and he could be distracted by almost anything. It was no easy task for his teacher, but she was unusually sympathetic and did everything she could to help.

But Billy made things so difficult for her that by Christmas vacation of that year she had told her husband (who was principal) that unless Billy's behavior improved significantly, she couldn't keep him in her class. Happily, Billy did seem to improve when school started again in January and so was able to continue throughout that school year. That was the first of several situations in which Billy seemed just barely to hang on with his schooling. We felt deeply grateful to the faculty and administration for what we knew was a great deal of extra trouble and effort on their part.

Those first months in Chicago were difficult ones for Helen. She still hadn't fully regained her health, and the tension of coping with Billy in a new situation was sometimes severe and trying.

I was busy with pastoral duties in a large congregation, often away from the house. Caring for four small children, she was seldom free of responsibilities. And the extra concern of Billy's unpredictability kept her on edge. She had to struggle to keep him under control in church services, while I was leading the congregation in worship. She had to iron out the squabbles that arose when Billy annoyed or was teased by the children in the neighborhood. And because of his behavior, it was more of a strain than a pleasure to take him anywhere with us.

Some in the congregation sensed the problem and gave us just the lift we needed. I think especially of Steve and Charlotte. They had known the heartbreak of seeing their son die of leukemia at the age of seven. Their hearts went out to Billy, who was at that exact age when he came to Chicago. When we visited in their home, we knew that they understood and we were comforted beyond words. From time to time Charlotte would drop in and offer to take Billy to their home for a few hours, always at times when Helen needed relief the most. And others helped, too. We felt more and more that the congregation was with us in our struggle, and that made us appreciate them all the more.

During that first winter in Chicago, about six months after the onset of his illness, Billy's seizures began. At first they were very minor. We noticed how at times the expression on his face would grow blank. He seemed for a time not to see. The doctors told us that scar tissue was forming where brain injury had occurred from the high fevers, and that we could perhaps expect more abnormalities of this kind. And they were right.

The most alarming development was his tendency to fall during a seizure. I can remember seeing him play outside on a winter day. Suddenly, without apparent warning, his body grew rigid, his right arm was extended, and he fell backward stiffly to the ground. Once, this even happened on the steps of the front porch.

He never was seriously injured in a fall, though we lived with a half-conscious fear that he might. Gradually, the seizures were brought under control through medication. He continued to have them, but they were less frequent and less severe. After he began taking a medication regularly, his seizures usually involved only a jerking of his head and a momentary stiffening of his right side.

In the midst of all this, however, our hopes were still high that Billy would eventually recover. Often I would go into his room at night after he was asleep and put my hands on his head, praying for his recovery. There were others in our congregation who were physically afflicted and Billy's condition seemed to give us intense feelings for them. There was Bobby, who also suffered from epileptic seizures. There was Bill, whose back condition made it impossible for him to work or even to come to church. Helen and I would pray, sometimes with tears, that God would reveal his power and compassion in healing these and others. Months wore on and no striking changes were evident. And yet somehow it still seemed right to pray.

We accepted his affliction without becoming resigned to it. We knew that God's hand was in it, and yet we felt that there was much more ahead in his purpose for Billy. How can you keep on praying with faith when months stretch into years, and the answer simply doesn't seem to come? I don't know exactly how. I can simply say that it is possible and that to us it seemed most fitting. We found releasing and renewed hope in spreading Billy's needs before a gracious Lord.

We discovered later that we were repressing many feelings about the situation. And however well we as parents seemed to be adjusting to everything, it was plain that Dave and Jimmy were finding it difficult.

Dave, for example, had to learn an entirely new role in the family. Before that day in June, Billy had been his big brother, his leader, his commander-in-chief. But now, though still physically larger, Billy could neither lead nor defend. Instead of having a big brother on whom he could depend, Dave suddenly found himself as Billy's supervisor, checking on him to be sure he came home from school, and in many other things. If there was a leader among the boys, now it had to be Dave. He had to do a lot of growing up in these first few months.

Jimmy, on the other hand, had to bear a good deal of torment from his oldest brother. Billy seemed frustrated by his limitations and sometimes he vented that frustration on his brothers. Since Dave could take care of himself fairly well, and since Jonny as the baby enjoyed more adequate protection, Jimmy wound up taking much of the abuse. He found some relief by retreating to his chemistry lab in the cedar closet.

The atmosphere in which the brothers spent those years could hardly be called carefree. They all felt hurt by the change in Billy and by the hostility he seemed to feel toward them. They often complained with pain in their eyes and wished almost bitterly that Billy had never been sick. At times they were impatient with us because we didn't discipline him more severely. The body of the family had a stricken, throbbing member, and all of us were feeling the pain.

Summer, 1960, was a healing time for us all. The church in Chicago had generously given me all of July and August as vacation time so that I could work on my doctoral dissertation at Princeton Seminary. I had made arrangements early in the spring to rent a large, lovely old home in Hightstown, New Jersey, for the summer.

The house was surrounded by tall hedges. It had spacious grounds behind it on which stood a barn and several smaller buildings. Part of it was almost like a forest. Our boys had never known open space like this, either in Lodi or in Chicago. They reveled in it. A huge collie dog and a tribe of cats made the rustic setting complete.

Each morning I took along a lunch that Helen had packed and drove to Princeton to spend the day in the library. When I arrived home each day shortly before supper time we had the evening to ourselves as a family. No meetings, no church visitation, no emergency calls—these were the most relaxing days that we had known since we were married. Almost every evening we drove through an abandoned World War II defense plant, seeing how many rabbits and pheasants we could scare up in the process.

Billy seemed easier to manage. In Hightstown he had plenty of space and no near neighbors. He enjoyed exploring the grounds and playing with cats, and he joined with enthusiasm in our family ball games each evening.

And, for the first time since her illness, Helen had the time and strength to give Billy some much-needed teaching. He had learned to print in the first grade, but he had made no progress in writing script. Day after day, with remarkable patience, she labored with him until by the end of summer he could do a fair job of writing. This was the most significant stride he had taken in his education since the previous summer. Though sometimes impatient at the need to practice, he was proud of his accomplishment. Needless to say, so were we.

Toward the end of the summer, when Billy seemed so manageable, we grew brave—brave enough to invite Dr. Otto Piper and his wife to dinner in our home. Dr. Piper, a noted New Testament scholar, was my advisor in the doctoral program at Princeton Seminary. Billy was hardly a model child while the Pipers were with us, but it was wonderful to see how they understood his problem. We found ourselves comfortable in talking it over with them.

By the end of the summer we were immensely refreshed and encouraged. I had made good progress on my dissertation. Helen was feeling like her former self. The boys were healthy and happy, and Billy seemed ready for a good year. We returned to Chicago with grateful hearts and high hopes.

Billy's second year at Roseland Christian School was in some respects like the first. Once again, he had an understanding teacher. In some areas, such as arithmetic and oral reading, he continued to do work that was at or above his third-grade level. His overall performance was not quite as good, however, when measured by the rest of the class. What had been Bs on his report card became Cs, and he continued to have problems in relating to the other children, as well as in following the classroom routine.

Although the school was only three and a half blocks from our home, Billy's transportation to and from school became something of a problem. Dave and Jimmy were reluctant to walk with him on the way to school, and on the way home, whether intentionally or not, he developed a rather regular habit of getting lost. Often we solved the problem by driving him there and back again, but sometimes that was impossible. We spent some highly anxious hours in search of a wandering boy.

When Billy was not in school he found trouble occupying himself. His crippled right side made it increasingly difficult for him to compete with the other boys in sports. He soon lost interest or compensated for his handicap by spoiling the game for the others. Younger children in the neighborhood came to fear his left-handed attacks. Alternately restraining and protecting him came to be almost a full-time job.

During this year he formed a habit of wandering into local stores. There was a small grocery store several houses down from us on 107th Street and a pharmacy just around the corner on Michigan Avenue. Both of these he frequented and began pilfering candy bars and other small items. He was anything but subtle in this, and his crimes were always detected.

But the fact that it was happening increased our sense of frustration. How can you handle a boy like Billy, short of watching him every moment? With his impulsive, unpredictable behavior, what is there to keep him from getting into real trouble?

Physically, his condition showed little change. He was still receiving regular therapy and now was walking without a brace. But his walk had stabilized at a slight limp and dropping of the foot, and he still could not use his right hand.

The seizures were fairly well controlled, but during one of the practices for the Sunday school Christmas program Billy "blacked out" and fell. The lady who was directing the program brought him to us, and we all decided it was best that he not try to participate in the program. It was not a major thing in itself, but it seemed one more door closing between Billy and the normal life we longed to see him have.

That year with our congregation was a busy, happy one. We grew to appreciate them more and more and were glad to see evidences that our ministry of the gospel was bearing fruit. But Billy's situation kept things tense under the surface and by July we were more than ready for another two months in Hightstown.

5

A Family Crisis

After we had moved to Chicago, Helen typed letters to our families in New York and Georgia for a number of years. Carbon copies of these letters, along with Bill's journal entries, preserved much of the history of those years. We have combined our stories in what follows.

By the time we returned from New Jersey in late August of 1961, Bill's dissertation was nearing completion and we all felt fairly rested. Although we didn't realize it at the time, the school year beginning that September was to be Billy's last in his school. Each month his difficulties in school had seemed to increase slightly, and we sensed before many weeks of the fall term had passed that more serious problems were ahead. We lived from one minor crisis to another in Billy's school life. We marveled at the patience and fortitude of his teachers.

As the school year progressed, Dave, Jimmy, and little Jonny began to show signs of increased strain. Except when Billy was at school or asleep, there were few relaxed moments in our home. One weekend old friends from Lodi stayed in our home for a few days. Just before leaving they spoke to us frankly about what they had observed while among us. "Something has to be done about

Billy," they said. "It's just too hard on the rest of the family. It's as if a dark cloud were over your home."

That really made us think. We had sensed a vague awareness of impending trouble, but living right in the situation we couldn't observe the changes as well as a visitor could. Now we began to wrestle with the matter more urgently. But nothing seemed to open up.

In the spring of 1962 we were more severely jolted. Bill was in his study at the church preparing for an evening meeting when the phone rang. It was Helen. Terror was in her voice. "Billy's been hit by a car at the corner of State and Wabash! A little girl rushed to our home to tell me. Will you go?" Bill tore out the back door and sprinted the block and a half to State Street, heart pounding. A small crowd had gathered. By the time Bill got there, Billy was sitting on the curb. He looked up at Bill with a frightened look in his eyes, but Bill saw that he wasn't badly hurt. "Are you all right, Billy?"

"Yeah."

Moments later the ambulance arrived and whisked him to a hospital for examination. No broken bones, hardly even a bruise. Thank God!

On his way home from school Billy had come as far as State Street and hadn't noticed that the light was red. He had limped out into the street, right into the flow of traffic. Fortunately, the lady in the blue Chevrolet saw him coming. She pumped the brakes frantically and skidded to a stop, just as her car reached him. The impact was scarcely enough to knock him off his feet. The driver was unnerved, deeply concerned about Billy. When word came that he was all right, all of us were vastly relieved, grateful for God's protecting hand, and for a woman's presence of mind.

But afterward we couldn't get the accident out of our minds. Billy had been spared, but there would be other days, other street corners, other impulsive blunders. How could he stay in school? Who could be watching him every moment? What would happen next?

As we inquired about possibilities or the future, a psychologist told us about a book named *The Other Child*, which described Billy's condition and schools to help such children: Cove School in Wisconsin. We devoured the book. On page after page we found ourselves saying, "That's Billy!" The impulsiveness, the unpredictability, the brief attention span, the seizures, the mystifying mixture of keen intelligence and inability to learn—all of it was there. We felt that a kind of weight had been lifted from our spirits. There were other children like Billy whose brain damage had the same puzzling effects! And what was more, here were people who understood Billy and knew how he could best be helped. We were elated and took steps immediately to have him enrolled at Cove. This school focused on the special needs of brain-injured children.

We went there to visit and liked what we saw. The school occupied one of the buildings of what had been a large monastery near Lake Michigan. It had been started by a doctor and was now being headed by his widow and another physician. They told us about "the other child," about the behavior of brain-injured children and the special problems they face. In the fall of 1962, the whole family drove up to Wisconsin to take Billy there.

We had been trying to prepare him for weeks. He had visited the school earlier, had been shown around the buildings, and had seemed content with the idea of staying there, but when the time came, how hard it was for him to be left behind! For years his problems had filled every day with struggle and anxiety, but we felt empty and guilty about sending him away. We signed all the necessary papers, got him settled in his room, walked for awhile around the grounds, and then got ready to head back to Chicago. Billy showed little emotion at the time, but there was a plaintive look in his eyes as we gave him a goodbye hug. It was a long, sad drive back home. We tried to cheer each other with the thought that this was best for all of us. And it was.

We noted an almost immediate change in the atmosphere around our home. The boys asked about Billy, wondered how he was doing, remembered him in their prayers; but the daily pressure of his problems had been lifted from them. Something of their joy and spontaneity came back. We were glad for them and were reassured that we had done the right thing.

Cove School, as we had learned at the outset, was an expensive proposition. The monthly cost for Billy's room, board, and tuition was quite a sum in the early sixties. My salary each month hardly matched that figure, but our congregation rallied around us. When a number of families in the church wanted to help us financially, some dear friends coordinated the effort. Each month I gave as much as I could toward Billy's expenses and they saw to it that the rest was provided. Through all of the two years that Billy was in Cove, we were always extended financially, but the bills were always paid, thanks to those generous friends.

One especially notable gift came from members of our first congregation in Lodi, New Jersey. The husband had had a wonderful conversion experience while we were there. He and his wife had felt God's call to enter the ministry even though he was almost fifty at the time. He called himself an "eleventh-hour laborer." He had made it through seminary and with characteristic energy had thrown himself into the work of his first pastorate. The costs of education had drained their savings and they were living very modestly, but during the year that Billy went to Cove School, they sent us a magnificent gift at Thanksgiving to help with his expenses! It was such an overwhelming act of love that we hardly knew how to respond.

For Billy the first year at Cove was difficult. In spite of a good deal of individual attention, he made little progress in his school work. He was hyperactive, easily distracted, a constant problem in class. He laughed loudly, teased other children, sometimes even kicked and tripped them. He had been given the most extensive tests and was being supervised by experts, but there were few changes for the better. And he missed his home.

We had been advised when we left him in the fall not to return for a few weeks so that he could become adjusted to his life at Cove School. When we finally made our first visit, we felt sick at heart. As we came in to greet him, all smiles, Billy burst into tears. He didn't like "that place." He wanted to "go home." After a few hours with us he felt better. We took him down to the lakeside and let him throw stones out into the water. We had brought him some trinkets that he liked, and some new baseball cards.

But as we were ready to leave, the tears flowed again. We began to have doubts. Was this really helping Billy? Even at this ideal place, with so much help available, was he going to get better? We had heard reports of other brain-injured children who had made great progress at Cove School, but Billy's record so far was disappointing. We spent time during each visit learning about Billy from the officials there. Their input always proved helpful.

By the spring of 1963 the situation looked brighter. Billy had been passing through a rapid growth spurt and seemed to be calming down. Cove School didn't operate during the summer months, so Billy would be home with us again for June, July, and August. We were happy for that. It had been a long, long year—for him and for us, and we looked forward to his return. His brothers were happy, too. They had almost forgotten the pain and frustration of his years at home.

But now it was to begin again. Billy didn't have the former perils and troubles of school, but living in that part of Chicago during a hot summer had its problems for him. He had developed quite a throwing arm and threw numerous objects through the parsonage windows. The first time or two we reported it to the board of deacons, and they arranged to have the glass replaced. After that we were too embarrassed to ask. It seemed simpler to have the windows fixed ourselves and say nothing about it. We kept the glass companies going that summer.

But just when the tensions were building up with other children around the neighborhood, we drove out East to visit Helen's parents. It was the break we all needed. Billy was hard to manage on the road, but we were able to keep enough distance between him and the others boys in our station wagon to maintain a semblance of peace.

When fall came we prepared to take Billy, now eleven years old, to Cove School again. Though it had been a hard summer, we had hopes for a better year ahead. As we talked to Billy about going back, he consented, but we had the feeling that he didn't really grasp what was about to happen. When the day arrived, he didn't want to go. Once there, we again had trouble leaving him.

The second year at Cove was to be a happier one for Billy. He made a much better adjustment to his environment and got along more amicably with the other students. He became noticeably quieter and less belligerent. He began to blossom as a person—a joy to be around. His learning problems continued and the atrophy on his right side became more noticeable, but he seemed to be more at peace.

We brought Billy home for several weekends during that year and took him several times to a Chicago branch of the Institute for the Development of Human Potential. This institute promised new hope for the brain-injured. It had long been known that brain damage is irreversible. Brain cells, once destroyed, do not replace themselves.

These doctors theorized, however, that brain development in a child occurs in connection with bodily movement. A child's brain grows, for example, as he passes through the stages of creeping and crawling. Perhaps if the movements of those early years could be artificially reproduced for those who had been paralyzed through brain injury, some new brain development might be stimulated. It was essentially an attempt to "program" the brain. At the heart of the procedure was what was called "patterning." At regular intervals each day, five persons were to give the child a patterning exercise, one moving each of the legs and arms, and one turning the head. We heard startling reports of restored function among those who had used this patterning process for several months. We listened; we learned; we were convinced it was worth trying.

While all this was happening, a new possibility opened for our ministry. Bill was invited by the board of Western Theological Seminary in Holland, Michigan, to serve there as Professor of Preaching. It was difficult for him to leave a pastorate in which he had found much joy and fulfillment, but he had always felt a deep concern for the equipping of ministers. In pursuing his doctoral studies, he had often considered the possibility of seminary teaching. This invitation from Western seemed to us to be God's call. As Billy finished his second year at Cove School, we brought our ministry to a close in Chicago. In July the whole family moved to the Tulip City: Holland, Michigan.

6

First Years in Michigan

As we looked for a place to live in Holland, Billy's safety was a primary concern. The staff at Cove School had advised us that he was ready to live at home now. We were ready for that, too, but we needed the right kind of neighborhood setting. One potential danger was automobile traffic. The memory of that near tragedy on State Street was very much with us. We decided against two or three houses because, although they were adequate in other respects, they were located by heavily traveled streets, or near the lake. Finally, we found what seemed the ideal place. The home was on a one-block street so that there would be no through traffic. Directly across from it was a large playground. It was on the southern side of Holland, almost at the city limits.

Other questions about the neighborhood were more difficult to answer. How would the neighbors react to Billy's presence on their street? How would other children relate to him? It looked like a fine environment for Billy, but how would he fit in?

It proved to be a good neighborhood for Billy. The people who lived there couldn't have been more kind and understanding. Our neighbors on both sides and the family behind us all welcomed us warmly. After they had begun to know us and

Billy, they seemed relaxed to have him around. And he, for his part, was much calmer than before. He had room to roam around the neighborhood, and a large playground in which to play. His brothers were old enough now to cope with him. He seemed to adjust well to his new surroundings. We felt greatly relieved.

In the fall of 1964 Billy began attending an elementary school about a mile from our home. His final evaluation at Cove School had suggested that he be placed in a room for physically handicapped and perceptually impaired children. A nearby school in Holland had such facilities. The year proved to be difficult, but Billy survived, and so did we!

During our first years in Holland, we were members of a church where the pastor and his wife had been dear friends of ours for many years. We had corresponded and shared concerns many times while we were in Chicago and he in Grand Rapids, and now it was good to be together, serving in the same city. This congregation welcomed us warmly and showed real interest in Billy. When we decided to embark on the patterning program of exercise recommended by the Institute for the Development of Human Potential, we were profoundly moved by the response of the church people. Almost two hundred of them volunteered to help!

The patterning was to be done five times a day and it took five people to participate each time. Scores of people coming to our home every week to exercise a brain-damaged boy! Students at the seminary and other friends of the family joined the corps. Billy was less than enthusiastic about being patterned so often, but he enjoyed the attention immensely. The social stimulus it provided was like a tonic for him. It was the high point in his day when some of his favorite people arrived to give him a workout. Great was the chatter and hilarity as we moved his arms and legs and head back and forth, simulating the technique of creeping.

All three of his brothers took part, as well as his parents. We five, when necessary, could pattern him ourselves, and we often did when we were traveling or, for one reason or another, some of the helpers couldn't come. For almost an entire school year we continued that daily regimen. We don't know that Billy gained much movement on his right side as a result, but the exercise was surely beneficial and the daily contact with interested and loving people enriched him beyond words to express.

One of Billy's special benefactors was Dale. He and Mary operated a local business and were active members of our church. They took on the responsibility of being with Billy during the Sunday-school hour. We hadn't been able to find a class that was right for him, and we were at a loss to know what he could do while the rest of the family was in Sunday school. Each Sunday Dale and Mary took him for a ride, sometimes sightseeing, sometimes to visit their home, sometimes just to talk. He always came back from those outings happy and often with some little gift. Dale and Mary were chief among many kind people who brightened Billy's early days in Holland.

Junior high school seems to be a trying period for many young people. It certainly was so for Billy. When he moved to E.E. Fell Junior High School, an old brick building near the center of Holland, he was placed in the special education room. His learning problems had now become more apparent and each year he fell a little further behind his grade level. From time to time we were called in for conferences with his teachers. He had difficulty concentrating and was sometimes a disruptive influence in class. Worse still, some of the young people in the class, which consisted of the physically handicapped, the mentally retarded, and the culturally deprived, found Billy's combination of handicaps offensive. Not daring to hurt him, they sometimes vented their frustration on his younger brother, Dave.

One afternoon we received an urgent call from the junior high school office. When we arrived we found Dave in the principal's office, sobbing uncontrollably. He had been cornered and beaten by two of the older boys in the special education class. He hardly knew them. When he asked why they were tormenting him, their answer was, "Because your brother is a mental." The beating had been hard enough to take, but that made it almost unbearable. Anger, pain, and bitterness came pouring out of Dave for hours afterward. It hurt us to see him suffer so, and our hearts were pained when we saw him pound his head against the pillow of his bed, saying, "I can't believe in any God who would let that happen to my brother!" That was the first expression of painful doubting which was to afflict Dave's life for several years. Billy's illness had been a blow to all of us, but especially so to Dave. It was hard for him to accept the crippling illness that had turned a beloved big brother into a source of embarrassment and trouble.

Often it seemed to us that Billy's junior high school years brought one crisis after another. We were happy when he was finally graduated into what we hoped would be better facilities and a more adequate special education program at the local high school. We still felt thankful for his supportive junior high teachers, however, who had hung in with Billy through difficult days.

7

High School Days

From Bill

High school was a fresh start for Billy. From a cramped, downtown junior high school, he had moved to a beautiful, spacious campus. It was exciting for him to be around "the big kids," especially those who were active in high school athletics. We had high hopes that in this new environment his school work would improve.

That, however, didn't seem to happen. He liked the special education class and got along well with his teachers, but it was hard for us to discover what he was learning. One day he told us that he had been working on the names of the states of the union. He would recite almost all of them. That seemed encouraging, but several weeks later when we asked him what he was doing in class we got the same response. He was learning the names of the states! We began to feel that something wasn't ideal. He had his learning problems, we were sure of that, but it seemed that he should be working on something more useful and substantial.

We tried to find out what we could about the curriculum in that special education class. It was hard to get a clear impression about it. The special education department seemed to be understaffed, and the man who was Billy's chief teacher was carrying a heavy load of responsibilities outside the school. Our uneasiness grew.

By the end of that school year, Billy's future in school had become questionable. The special ed teachers weren't sure that high school, even in a special education class, was the place for Billy. The problem lay in his seizures. It was unsettling to the staff, they said, and to the other students that Billy would sometimes black out and fall. Some feared that he might be seriously injured.

And although his relationship with his fellow students had improved, he was still a distracting influence in class. He had picked up a couple of phrases which he repeated with wearisome frequency: "Shut up" and "I don't care!" These were his stock responses to his fellow students and even occasionally to his teachers. The possibility we had feared seemed about to happen. It was suggested that a home-bound program might be easier for Billy—a teacher coming to the house periodically while his mother worked with him to supplement the program.

We knew that wasn't the answer. Billy needed desperately his social contacts at the high school. To keep him at home would have been to deprive him of many opportunities for personal growth. It was hard for us to fight back the gloom. Was this the end of the road for Billy's schooling? Helen sought out the superintendent to plead Billy's case. She offered to help if there was any way Billy could remain in school.

At the same time, there were changes going on in special education in the high school. One of the teachers had left and a replacement was being sought. The school authorities asked Helen, knowing of her previous teaching experience, if she would like the job as a permanent substitute. She said that she would be delighted to accept, provided Billy could remain in school. They agreed to that and the next fall Helen became Billy's regular classroom teacher. She had to go back to school for her certification, and eventually for a master's in special education, but she was allowed to do this while continuing as an active teacher.

We were overjoyed. This was more than we had dared to hope for. Not only was Billy still in school, but Helen was right there with him, in his classes. One more crisis had been passed, and once again there was hope for Billy's education. He was beginning to show more mature behavior.

Two things stand out for us as especially memorable during Billy's junior year in high school. First, he made confession of faith in Jesus Christ. Growing up in a minister's home, Billy had been exposed to the Christian gospel from the time of his birth. We had been singing the hymns of the faith from the time he could first talk. But from the time of his illness onward it was hard to determine how much of the faith he understood. When we asked him an occasional question about it, he either said, "I don't know" or gave back a rote, almost mechanical answer. When he prayed aloud at the table, he seemed to shift his speech into high gear. A few familiar phrases came out so close together as to be almost indistinguishable.

As time went on, however, his interest and responsiveness to spiritual matters seemed to grow. Occasionally he asked a question that showed some reflection. During his junior year he decided to become part of the pastor's class at our church. He attended all the sessions, appeared before the elders, and was received one Sunday morning with a number of other young people as a communicant member of the church. I remember asking him that day about what this step had meant to him. What a joy I felt at his responses!

"What did Jesus do for you, Bill?"
"He died for my sins."

"Did he stay dead after that?"
"No, he rose from the dead."

"And where is he living now, Bill?"
"In my heart."

Billy had a peculiar way of answering such questions. His answers would be somewhat tentative, with a slight rising inflection as though it were a question, and he would look at me as if to discover whether he had said the right thing. We never knew just how much of the good news of Jesus Christ he clearly grasped, but he seemed to trust in Jesus with an untroubled, utterly child-like faith.

The second highlight of that year was Billy's position as assistant manager of the varsity basketball team. From his early childhood Billy had been a lover of sports. Until the time of his illness he was an enthusiastic participant. From that time onward he was to be mainly a spectator, but the enthusiasm still remained, or was greater than ever. The greatest joy of his week was to watch some kind of athletic event, either at Hope College or at the high school. Basketball seemed to hold a special attraction for him, perhaps because his younger brothers were so interested in it and perhaps because he could practice it by himself.

In our back yard, we had invested in a huge cement patio, only with us it wasn't a patio at all. It was a neighborhood basketball court. There Dave and Jim and Jon sharpened their skills, and there, when the court was available, Billy played his own private game, dribbling and shooting with his left hand. He became amazingly accurate, even to the point of beating his brothers occasionally in a game of "horse." When that happened he could hardly contain his delight and his brothers never heard the end of it.

Don, the high school basketball coach, knew about Billy's keen interest in athletics. Although he knew some of the problems that might be involved and didn't actually need another manager, he took on Billy as an assistant. What a thrill! Billy was given tasks like passing out the towels and picking up orange peels, which to him was always something of a lark. But the great thing was that he sat with the team and rode on the bus to the away games. The team members liked him, joked with him, and rushed to help him up when he fell.

How excited Billy was at the games! He had to be there early with his special sport jacket on, and when the team came running out on the court, Billy was limping along right behind them. That high school has never had a more ardent, loyal fan. He didn't cheer when the home team scored, but in his own special way he clapped. With his left hand he slapped his lame right wrist until it was red.

Helen writes to her family about Billy's basketball experience.

March 25, 1969

This Tuesday night we are going to attend the big basketball banquet. Billy is quite excited about this. Bill will have the invocation, and we are looking forward to a good time as well as the opportunity to say "thank you" to the team for all they have done to give Billy a sense of importance and worth.

March 30, 1969

Our basketball banquet Tuesday night was great. Billy said when he got home, "Mom, this was the biggest thrill I've ever had, to stand up in front of all those people with my team. I've never had anything like that happen to me before!" Billy seldom made comments like that. We were moved. Many parents spoke to us telling how much it meant to the team to have him—how they would never be the same again. The coach told him afterward that he wanted him back next year, and that, too, thrilled him. He tells everyone, "Did you know the coach wants me back again?" The other day we had a big assembly in the field house. As the kids were leaving, Billy fell. Students began to scatter, but then along came a basketball player. He grabbed him, picked him up, and said, "Here you go, Bill—okay?" This means so much to Billy—someone always ready to give him a hand, and not begrudging it either.

June 8, 1969
The coach came into the teacher's lounge the other day and asked me if Billy would like to work with the summer basketball league and be manager during the summer. You can imagine Billy's joy. This is the same league that Dave will be playing in, so that will be nice for him, too. I so appreciate the coach's interest in Billy. It is wonderful. I have been asked to continue teaching next year, and I feel I probably will. Billy has done so well that I'd hate to leave the work for his sake alone. I administered oral reading tests this past week to all the students, and I was thrilled to see all their progress. Billy was no exception.

After his birthday that fall, Helen wrote:

September 10, 1969
Billy was thrilled, as usual, to receive so many birthday remembrances. It hardly seems possible that he is 17 years old. He is on a full day schedule this year, and we're hoping it will go well. Bill bought him field glasses to watch football games for his birthday, and is he ever happy! I am so glad Bill thought of it.

Helen describes another rich experience for Billy in October:

I just finished helping Billy with an English assignment for the class he takes with other seniors. He seems to be getting along okay in it. He loves being in the boys' glee club, too. For that they wear dress tuxedos with red cummerbunds for their performance. And he will be doing that on December 14 for a big Christmas Vespers program. He is quite excited about it. The teacher excused him Thursday from class, and used the occasion to tell the other boys about Billy's seizure problem and what they should do were anything to happen during a performance. He said it was a tremendous class in which the boys showed such interest and concern for Billy that he was deeply moved. As we've said so often, it is

amazing how his problems and situation open up hearts—much more, I am sure, than had his life not been touched by tragedy. He got all spruced up this week with a barber's hair cut so that he could go to the studio and get his senior pictures taken. The photographer was very good with him, and we think he got some of the best pictures Billy has ever had taken since his illness.

By January of the next year, Helen wrote that physical problems for Billy were surfacing again:

January 4, 1970

Billy did not have a very good week. He was having such difficulty walking, his legs buckling out from under him, that we finally took him to the doctor. I was feeling pretty low about him and missing the prayers of Mother for him, too [Helen's mother had died December 12, a month before]. The doctor told us that we shouldn't have tried to have him run so much around the block, especially after he hadn't been used to it. Because his right leg is weak anyway, this extra exercise caused severe muscle weakness and he said his legs were just tired. Also, he told us that Billy is probably over-medicated, and that this causes his lack of stability. So we will reduce his medicine a little bit. He recommended rest for him, also. Already, in two days he is so much better that I guess the doctor was right. He'll be ready for school tomorrow, I am sure.

That March, we were looking toward a program of evaluation for Billy after his graduation. Helen writes:

March 14, 1970

Billy met with the vocational rehabilitation man this week, and the machinery was begun for him to qualify for the program of evaluation. We are going to try to work it out for him to go to this evaluation at the same time Bill goes to his pastoral counseling program this summer.

Billy's graduation from Holland High School was another exciting experience, in more ways than one, as Helen wrote in a June letter.

During practice in the morning he had fallen off the stage [a seizure] and had been rushed by ambulance to the emergency room of the hospital for stitches. Despite all this, Billy's graduation went off very well. There were no complications, and he was as proud as a peacock. He got fifty-two dollars in gifts alone plus some other presents, and he relished all the extra attention. The president of the Board of Education gave him a special handshake of congratulations—the only one in the graduating class of 350 seniors. He sat on the stage with the class president and the student body president. He looked and acted great. We felt thankful for it all, and a great sense of victory that he could make it this far.

8

Billy Goes to Work

From Bill

After Billy's graduation, he was able to begin the evaluation process for admission to the work program. We had high hopes for this. Here's another excerpt from Helen's June letter to her family.

Today was Billy's first day for evaluation and he left in great spirits this morning with his dad. Bill spent a little time yesterday getting the lay of the land for Billy, finding out just how it would go for him, and in making other arrangements so that he can start right in today. We are so thankful that it works out for them to go in together. Bill feels it will be a wonderful experience for Billy, and among other things, doctors will be observing his seizure problems in order to better balance his pills, too.

After some days, however, those working with Billy decided that he would not qualify for the work program there. We were discouraged, and felt painful concerns about his future.

Soon I was involved in a clinical pastoral education program there for the summer. I was part of one of the small groups involved in ministry to various patients. After several weeks, the leader of the entire program asked if I would speak at a meeting of all the groups—on any subject I chose. Since our disappointment over Billy was so recent, and had been much on my mind, I decided to tell them about our experience with this dear handicapped son.

There were about forty-five people present when I began to speak of Billy's struggles and our present sadness. What I did not know was that the meeting had been set up as an experiment—to see what happens to a communicator when no one listens!

As I told of Billy's illness and resultant handicaps, the group showed no interest. They did not seem to be listening at all. Some chatted with each other. Some looked downward or out the window. Some laughed or smirked. As I tried to tell our story, I felt myself dying on the inside. Just then I spotted one curly-haired student in my group who apparently sensed what was happening. He didn't go along with the plan, but gave me his full attention. So, looking right at him, I was able to finish. Afterwards, the leader was profusely apologetic, saying he had never dreamed that I would speak of something so poignant and personal. But I learned on that day how priceless it is to find someone who truly listens!

A few days afterward, in a meeting of our smaller group, I was asked how Billy was doing. I spoke of his disappointment, and ours, but described it in a way that had become a mannerism for me—with a smile. Our leader, a very perceptive man, noticed this. He asked, "That smile of yours. Is that how you really feel about this?"

The question shook me. I suddenly realized how much I had bottled up inside of my real feelings about Billy's situation. I dropped my head and said, "No." Suddenly the tears came, floods of them. I wept and wept and wept.

Finally, exhausted, I heard the leader ask, "What do you think Jesus is saying to you now?" He set an empty chair before me. I sat there, listening for what the Lord's message to me might be. These words seemed to come: "I know you're hurting, Bill, and I hurt, too. But hang in there. Better days will come."

That experience brought a releasing in which I still celebrate. I had for years tried to be the strong one in our family trauma, wanting to cope and hold things together, out of touch with the vast reservoir of pain and loss I felt. Now it had come pouring out, and I felt deeply relieved. I think it helps me still to get in touch with the sorrows of others.

Soon those "better days" for Billy did come. Here's another paragraph from Helen's June letter.

Monday night we went to the Kandu parents' meeting and got some very good news about Billy. The Director of Kandu Industries, a sheltered workshop in Holland, asked us to remain afterwards, and then he informed us that Billy would be working three days a week starting October 13, four days a week after another month, and then five days a week by January 1. The hours will be from nine to two, and when he has adjusted to a five-day week, the hours will move from nine to five each day. Kandu is expanding here in Holland and they will soon move to a new building. We are thrilled for Billy and he is too. We feel so thankful to the Lord for so many answers to prayer regarding his situation.

So began a beautiful chapter in Billy's life, his labors in a sheltered workshop. Helen writes again after Billy's birthday.

September 6, 1970
Billy had a very happy 18th birthday. Since we changed the amount of his medication, he has been getting better every day with his walking, talking, and general alertness and brightness. He hardly seems like the same boy. He was really excited and happy yesterday and very joyful over his gifts. It's been most encouraging to see him so well and strong, outside throwing balls, running, shooting baskets, and moving rapidly. We have an appointment for him in Chicago again

this year, October 22, and then we'll have a thorough drug evaluation. He is working two days a week here in Holland at Kandu Industries, and we're praying for an opening of this to a full-time thing soon.

September 20, 1970
Billy continues to be very good, and to work two days a week. They are expanding the work to a five-day work week here in Holland, but the details for this have not been worked out entirely with Kandu Industries. Billy should be working more before long, we hope.

By January of 1971, things were even better, as Helen writes:

Billy continues to enjoy his work and keeps busy with all his basketball games. He has been earning stars at work for two weeks solid for doing the best work of anyone at the plant. He is very proud of his productivity, and so are we!

That summer, we were able to enjoy a kind of ministry vacation together in Colorado, leaving our other sons in charge of Billy, and Helen writes:

July 1971
We had such a wonderful time in Colorado. I thanked Bill all the way back for making me go. The boys made out so well that Hilda, our neighbor, came over Saturday when we got back to tell me I sure had good boys! She said she couldn't imagine their car staying in the garage all week with the parents gone, but ours did! The boys never left Billy or Jonny alone, worked at their jobs so well that she said there was nothing for her to do when she came over to clean. I was really proud of them. Billy behaved very well for Dave and Jim, giving them no problem at all, and that was a great encouragement to us, too.

By his next birthday, we could see even more progress. Helen continues to write:

Labor Day 1971
Billy celebrated a very happy 19th birthday yesterday. These past few weeks have seemed especially good for him in a new level of maturity and thinking. Socially he seems to be really developing. With all the hardships, ups and downs, his life has certainly been a blessing and a joy for us. What he has contributed to our family has been really precious for us all. Dave was away for the weekend, but he came home to help him celebrate. That made Billy's day complete, since the sun rises and sets with Dave. As Dave says, "I sure get a lot of ego affirmation from Billy!"

Then, a month later,

October 10, 1971
With Dave and Jim helping out so much at home, it is easier for Bill to be gone. Dave took over completely for me with Billy, helping him to shave, etc. Jim ran the car pool for Jon's gang to junior high (we have that two mornings a week), so all in all the boys are a big boost to me.

Billy's 21st birthday, with some minor difficulties, was another great occasion.

September 23, 1973
Billy fell and had to have five stitches. We had open house at Kandu this past week. Over 2500 visitors went through the place and more contracts were obtained, too. Billy is leaving for work now at 7:30 and doesn't return until 4:00 in the afternoon, so he is really putting in quite a long day. He continues to be good, enjoying the college and high school football games these days, even though the White Sox disappoint him. I forgot to mention, he had a wonderful 21st birthday celebration on the 5th with about 24 people coming by with presents. He invited them all.

9

Billy's Greatest Moments

One of the most wonderful experiences of Billy's life came about through our friends, Max and Esther. Esther's brother is Jim Kaat, once an outstanding major league baseball pitcher. When our friends learned that Billy was a White Sox fan, they arranged for him to meet the great Jim Kaat at a baseball game in Comiskey Park, in Chicago.

Billy was beside himself with joy at the prospect. On the night of the game, we helped him down the stairs to the White Sox dugout. Out came Jim Kaat. He shook hands with Billy and presented him with a baseball autographed by all the Sox players. He gave him three extra balls! We took our cameras along and took pictures of Billy with his baseball hero. To top it off, Jim pitched the White Sox to a runaway victory that night. What a joy! The *Holland Sentinel* carried the whole story.

Our last family vacation with Billy was a trip to the Rose Bowl in 1976-77. Helen describes it in one of her letters.

January 8, 1977

Here is a hurried letter about our marvelous trip. We turned in our Buick for a car that is more economical and roomy. So our gas mileage went well and we were not too crowded in

the car. We had time going out to spend at the Grand Canyon and we enjoyed that even though we had to drive 120 miles out of the way. We also stopped at the Petrified Forest and the Painted Desert.

We had beautiful accommodations at the Hilton only two blocks from the parade route. We got a wheelchair for Billy so he wouldn't have to do quite so much walking. The shows were great at Disneyland and we spent the rest of the day there. Our hosts hired students to reserve seating on Colorado Boulevard for the parade. On Saturday morning we walked up to our padded folding chairs in the front row on the Boulevard and sat down.

After the parade (which was an experience in itself) we were escorted to the mansion overlooking the Rose Bowl stadium. There we were served a beautiful lunch and relaxed before walking down to the stadium and avoiding traffic hassles. The pageantry and excitement of being at the game was great. The crowds are unbelievable, but we had beautiful seats at the 40-yard line, 16 rows up from the field.

Even though Michigan lost, there was much that we enjoyed about the experience. The Michigan cheerleaders alone are worth being there to see. After the game we walked back up the steep hill from the stadium (by then Billy was tired and the boys practically dragged him back to the car).

We got back home Tuesday night and we all feel it was worth every minute of it. I'm sure we'll have memories that last a long time. Just the time to be with all the boys for a prolonged period was great. The time traveling flew with all our drivers and all our stimulating conversations and games in the car. We really had fun.

From Bill

Billy was the life of the party on our trip to California. Each of his college-age brothers was claiming to be the strongest, and angling for Billy's endorsement. He played his part artfully, encouraging first one, then another in their claims. During nights in a motel, Billy would snore prodigiously. The goal for his brothers (not often realized) was to fall asleep before he did.

After the loss to USC in the Rose Bowl game, Billy was disappointed—like all the rest of us. But his recovery was almost immediate. While we were still grousing and grumbling, he was his cheerful self again. All of us had to help him in the long walk back up the hill, but by the time we had struggled to the top, he had us laughing again. It was hard to stay down when we were around Billy.

Later that winter (1977) Helen and I planned a vacation time at Callaway Gardens, Georgia, with two other couples, long-time friends. When all efforts to have someone stay with Billy during that time didn't work out, we began to consider taking him along. Our gracious friends thought it would be a great idea, so he went with us. And what a time we had!

Billy seemed to enjoy every minute. He rode with me on the cart when we men played those beautiful Georgia golf courses. One day we got caught in a downpour, which Billy felt was great fun. As we careened through the wind and the rain he yelled at the top of his lungs with joy and excitement. We were so glad that he came along!

On the long, homeward drive, we had some memorable opportunities to talk with Billy. We spoke of suffering—what it meant. Did Billy think that he had ever suffered? His answer was swift and clear; a simple "No." We talked of faith in Jesus, and the future hope we have through him. Was Billy sure that he would be with Jesus at life's end? Again, no hesitation, "Yeah." "How can you know that for certain, Billy?" "Because I believe in Jesus." What a sunny spirit he showed on that journey home!

We had been back in Holland for a couple of days, getting settled. It was on Tuesday morning of Holy Week and Billy was scheduled to work at Kandu Industries. I heard him in the bathroom next to us about 6:00 a.m. I got up to see if he was all right. When he had just gotten out of his bed he was sometimes unsteady on his feet. I helped him back to his room and told him he could sleep for another hour. "I'll call you at seven," I promised.

For the next hour Helen and I were preparing for the day, having devotional times. My Bible reading for that morning was from the Gospel according to John, chapter 12. I was especially impressed by the verse: "Truly, truly, I tell you, unless a grain of wheat falls into the ground and dies, it remains just a single grain, but if it dies, it bears much fruit. Those who love their life lose it and those who hate their life in this world will keep it for eternal life." It struck me as a powerful theme often addressed by Jesus—fruitfulness out of losing ourselves, life out of death.

At 7:00 a.m. I opened Billy's bedroom door and was stunned by what I saw. He was lying face down on the carpet beside his bed. He didn't seem to be breathing, and when I held his wrist I felt no pulse. "Helen!" I cried, "come quick!" When she joined me in the room, I said, "Honey! I think Billy is dead."

We called 911 and our neighbors immediately. In a matter of minutes an emergency medical team had arrived. Heading it up was Kris, a young friend with whom I had played tennis. He felt our grief with us and spent several minutes in Billy's room, examining him for signs of life. Sadly, he rejoined us, shaking his head. "I'm afraid Billy has died. I'm so sorry."

From Helen

My reading that morning was from the passage I was studying in Philippians, chapter 4. I meditated on verses 4-7. God was speaking to me about my anxiety over Billy's seizures. Periodically he would fall in the midst of a seizure, and this would create desperate fear in me. When I would hear the sound of his falling somewhere in the house, my heart would pound and my stomach seemed to leap in my throat. I would say, "Please, Lord, let him be okay." Many times we had taken him to the emergency room for stitches, and once we came home to find a trail of blood all the way from the door to the couch where Billy was lying, calmly watching TV!

That Tuesday morning I thanked God first of all for our wonderful vacation with Billy. Then I sought to release my anxious thoughts about his seizures by committing the situation to the Lord in prayer, with thanksgiving.

At that startling moment in Billy's room, an amazing thing happened. Along with the shock and the sorrow, I was flooded with a great sense of peace. I felt God was somehow saying, "It is all right." I was overwhelmed. The heart throbbing, the stomach turning, the old anxiety—all gone. Instead I felt God's peace. Billy must have been taken in his sleep—with no falls or injuries. He was free at last, home at last. All was well. And God had prepared me through his precious Word!

I learned that morning that when you need peace, God provides it. We don't borrow trouble, but we can trust that when it comes, God will be there. I do not fear crises as once I did because God proved to me that day that when we pray with thanksgiving, handing our anxieties to the Lord, we will indeed find peace. Not ahead of time, but surely when the crisis comes.

Twenty-five years later, we wrote these postscripts:

From Helen

April 1, 2002 – Yesterday we celebrated Easter again. Twenty-five years ago Billy was buried on Easter Sunday. He has been in heaven longer than he lived on earth. As I reflect on those days and review those years, several thoughts surface for me:

As a mother and wife I was very busy, and during that time I probably ignored much of the pathos and pain that we lived through with a handicapped son. In some ways I feel more in touch with that pain now than when we were coping as a family all those years.

I am proud and grateful for the way we all coped and worked with each other as a family to manage a difficult time. We pulled together and tried hard to make our shared life workable and happy despite Billy's problems. The other boys demonstrated a maturity and capacity for caring far beyond their years.

God was very faithful to us. The whole experience did not lessen our trust in him and our belief that he would be with us in it.

Billy's illness began a huge change in my life in which I became an advocate for handicapped people. His behavior led to many occasions when I had to explain brain damage to a neighbor. Or I'd tell church members why Billy was hitting others in Sunday school. His shouting out in public demanded explaining, and his fighting with brothers led to important family conversations. I began to write and gathered the courage to send an article on handicapped persons to our church publication. The editor liked it and affirmed me, thus I became an author of sorts. This advocacy would develop into a career far beyond my wildest imagination.

I learned the meaning of service. As Billy's behavior became increasingly difficult, I started to experience depression over my parenting. I compared ours to other families where no problems seemed to exist. I had dreamed of being a Christian mother who would raise a wonderful family and prove an example to others. With Billy's problems, I began to wonder what people would think. One day I read in my devotions about our Lord coming "not to be served but to serve and to give his life . . ." The truth burst upon me that my calling was not to be personally successful, but to serve my family. I realized that I no longer should think of my reputation, but concentrate on taking up the cause of handicapped persons and loving them as our Lord did. I have become a stronger person, more able to understand and empathize with others who suffer.

From Bill

April 2, 2002 – Although his illness seriously diminished his powers, Billy's life really proved to be "for the praise of Christ's glory," both by his joyfulness in the midst of brokenness and in the blessed effects of his life on family and friends.

The healing for which we prayed has surely come, and we will celebrate it with him in the resurrection.

All of us were wounded by his affliction, but have become more compassionate and caring because of it.

The woundedness of our children has been our greatest sorrow, but the ways in which they have coped with it fills us with joy and gratitude.

God's ways are sometimes mysterious and painful to us, but he is ever faithful and gracious. Blessed be his name!

From son Jim,

in an article written about the same time (2002):

Why was Billy stricken? What was God's purpose in it? How were we now to live? What were we to do with our pain and loss? When I revisit those years in my memory, I encounter, from a child's view, the roots of the questions and assumptions that have followed me all my life. All that I have learned, for good or ill, of God's destiny, mercy, and call, begins here, with this story. Passing through the elementary grades, I was oblivious to much of this at the time. Children have an odd capacity to tune in and out of the radio frequencies on which the adult world communicates. I was vaguely aware of the turmoil but never really thought that I or our family was suffering. In a strange way, I thought it was normal to have a brother like Billy. It was not unusual that our family life would be disrupted as it was. Looking back now I see the river of sorrow and loss and the river of hope and longing that sustained us all in the midst of circumstances so painful that they would be utterly intolerable if they were not the same time so utterly ordinary and routinized. I see how closely sorrow is mingled with love, and how the river slowly, ever so slowly nourishes this broken world back to life.

Some days after Billy's death, Bill preached a message in his memory on Words of Hope. Here are excerpts from that message which was entitled "For Christ's Glory":

We are only beginning to realize the influence of Billy's life on us and on many others during the last few years. Here are some of the things his brothers have written about him. "Perhaps more than anything else, Billy was an admirer and a fan. He wrapped up his joys, hopes, and interests in the successes of those around him. Billy was like a mirror, taking our own delight and reflecting it back to us. Life was far richer simply because he was there. . ." Again, "Being with Billy gave me a sense of pride. Holding him up by his left arm while he entered church or a ball game was great. I never thought of spending time with Billy as a chore. He was a beloved brother. His simple life was a testimony to me of the joy of Christ which surpasses all knowledge."

One dear friend called us after Billy's death and said something like this: "If the grace which it brings to others is any measure of the significance of a human life, then Billy's was a significant life indeed." Yes, and that was all so effortless, and so unconscious on his part. He never had an inkling that he was exerting an influence on anyone (except as we told him so, at which his response invariably was, "Really?"). Billy ministered grace because he was so beautifully, transparently real. His was the heart of a child. He could be angry, but we never knew him to sulk. His range of activities was severely limited, but he was a stranger to boredom. How zestfully he lived! His laughter was boisterous, unrestrained. It seemed to come from deep inside him. I can see him now, head thrown back, eyes shining, his whole body shaking with mirth. He loved to be teased and to respond emphatically, "No way!" He found the most intense pleasure in little things.

Billy had mastered the high art of living in the present. He would pull for his favorite team with life and death urgency, but when the game was over and the cause was lost, he was completely without regrets. The rest of us might torment ourselves a while with, "If only this; if only that," but not Billy. It was over and he was happy in the present.

If he was in intense pain he would let us know, sometimes with a yell. But self-pity totally passed him by. The whine, the whimper, the brooding complaint; all that was unknown to him. He had a dozen infirmities that most of us never have to struggle with, but somehow he didn't *feel* afflicted or deprived. It wasn't simply that he rejected pity; it made no sense to him that anyone should extend it to him. He could smile and be of good cheer with his head bleeding, his hip fractured, or his right arm hanging useless at his side. He was at peace with the life God had given him.

After his death, letters, phone calls, personal words poured in about what he had meant to people. A man who had done more than almost anyone else in Holland to promote employment for the handicapped said that it was Billy's life that had awakened his interest. Many told us through their tears how his cheerful, childlike spirit had touched them. And we remembered that his own mother had become active in ministering to the handicapped and had been able to help hundreds of young people, largely because Billy had been in our home.

Reflecting on his life and witness leads me to three thoughts, and with these I close.

First, the really significant lives may not always be the ones that we consider important. We take note of those who have power and influence, remarkable gifts, great wealth, but do they give the most to others and to the world?

Second, God may not answer some of our prayers because he is busy answering our deepest prayer. The healing we asked for Billy never came in this life, but we are realizing more and more how he lived to the praise of God's glory.

And *last*, how good it is to know that if we are in Christ, no handicap, no frustration, no seeming tragedy can keep us from fulfilling God's purpose for our lives.

From Helen

Learnings that came to us as parents of a handicapped child:

- We needed a different approach to discipline for Billy. We found the best way to handle acting-out behavior was to give him time out in his room. We would let him be alone for a time away from stimulation while helping him to understand that this would settle him down.
- We recognized Billy's limitations in relating to his peers. We found more mature persons or adults to befriend him. We would explain the nature of his problem and invite them to be a friend to him.
- When Billy was suffering in a situation because he was different, we would ask the leader to explain (in Billy's absence)

why Billy was different and secure the help of the group to make him feel accepted.

- We discovered that a resource room was helpful. This is a place where Billy could be freed from having to achieve more than he was able. It was a place of respite, and it did not have to be permanent or involve more than one or two hours of class time. It enabled his teacher to be an advocate for him in other situations and classes.
- We did not keep Billy's limitations to ourselves. We discovered that openness and asking for the prayers of our friends proved helpful. We recognized that we could not carry the burden alone, and others appreciated our confiding in them. They also became advocates for Billy.
- We became advocates ourselves. We pled the cause of others who were different and prayed for them.
- We looked at alternative plans for Billy's future. We exposed our child to varied experiences in order to determine where he could best succeed.
- We gave our other children in the home relief from Billy from time to time. We often explained his handicap to them so they would understand why we managed him differently at times.
- We committed Billy to the Lord every day and allowed him to experience some things that involved risk. We tried to avoid the temptation to be overprotective.

10

Dave's Despair

The news of Billy's death was heart-wrenching for his brothers, especially for Dave. He, Jim, and Jon were then students at the University of Michigan, and they came home together. In our mind's eye, we can still see Dave, face contorted with grief, stumbling in our front door. He sat in a lounge chair in our living room, weeping bitterly. He couldn't seem to stop. The rush of tears went on and on, then a pause, then more. We had never seen anything affect Dave like this.

Here are some of his later reflections about his brother's death:

He died without a word. Leaving in joy, causing us pain. Precious in the sight of the Lord is the death of his saints.

Death has us all in a relaxed, yet timeless grip. Terrible, terrifying, trembling it seems to me. Unexpected—yes. Unsuspecting were we. There is a time to be born and a time to die. The wind blows where it will. So it is.

If only one could understand something of it all—just a part. It would be so much more satisfying. Unintelligible, insurmountable, immutable are his ways, it is said. Often—often.

Give me room, just a little space to stand clear, to perceive. I can't bear up under it at all. And I continue to reach, to stretch for something which can solve it all, or at least something.

"Come home right away—Billy's dead," they said. My head spun, my stomach tightened. Ill at ease, I laid myself vertically onto my bed. Then heaving and crying bitterly, I was no longer a stranger to grief. Home soon, I'm crying at my door. I'm crying inside, I'm crying on the outside. It's far too much to bear. And I break. Down, down, down, till I can't cry any more. Almost numb, I sway through the next few days grieving helplessly.

I can't help wondering sometimes. I shudder when I pause to remember the bright eyes, the atrophied arm. It is more or less a matter of perspective. And time changes all things.

Still I shudder at the thought of having known him and then lost him.

When several weeks later Dave graduated from the University of Michigan, he decided to spend that summer touring Europe and visiting R., a college friend from Germany. His journal entries during that time tell of his travel experiences and the beginning of a descent into mental illness.

May 19, 1977 – First stop: Germany – Today . . . to put it mildly, was a little on the rough side, almost a little scary for me, personally. Most of the day I was quite tired and felt rather weary. I had little energy. I felt a little crazy a good bit during the day. I spent some time trying to figure out why I felt so badly. I talked the whole subject over with R. in a most absurd way. I hypothesized that it was the change in diet and culture that was affecting me. I said I felt I needed more time to get adjusted. I think this may be true but I'm not entirely convinced. I have felt these things for the last several days, and have hoped that things would grow a bit better, but today they were worse. Being away from everything familiar has its advantages and disadvantages in coping with craziness.

May 20, 1977 – I am still living under a bit of a cloud. When will it clear? I'm striving for peace on all borders without and within. Can

I find it? I wish, I wish to fly away from it all. I wish for more poetry and song, less that is crass and untimely . . . I'm still striving for peace . . .

Five days later, no relief,

May 25, 1977 – Today was a good day in some ways, but absolutely horrible in other ways. I don't know where to begin. I'll start with what is so bad. I can't quite stand what is going on with me inside my head and around me here in Germany. I feel like I am going completely crazy a lot of the time. Maybe I am. I'm not sure. I think my better judgment and God's word to me tells me I am not and that I shouldn't be so concerned but I am almost increasingly. I don't know how to understand what is going on in me. It is very difficult . . . I must admit that a lot of these questions are running through my head and are a considerable source of difficulty for my general ability to cope with the foreign culture.

Dave describes his mental state in more detail.

June 22, 1977 – All the while I'm feeling worse and worse. I'm very tired for one thing. And this feeling of utter estrangement and falseness from my romantic dreams has quite overtaken me. I'm feeling tossed about without any place to land, and so it starts to affect me. I notice I can't maintain a reasonably high level of organization in playing the little geography game. I can't think of places or names as quickly as I once could or would like to. It's as if I am very foggy constantly and not able to break through with a clear and coherent thought. And it stays like this the whole time I'm sitting in this station waiting for the train. Anyway, there was no fighting off the creeping craziness. I tried everything, believe me. I prayed, talked, walked, and got very cold and I might add, reflected, tried to piece things together in my own mind, etc. but nothing seemed to fit, and my private thoughts just seemed to be crumbling away.

July 17, 1977 – My God, how I've lived through so much. I can't believe the kind of changes I seem to be going through either. I'm becoming very bourgeois and sedate. Revoltingly comfortable and unimaginative, good for about nothing creative. I think I've stopped learning and growing. I also think I've probably had something resembling a nervous collapse.

A complicating factor for Dave in Europe was uncertainty about his relationship with M (a girlfriend). He had traveled with her for some time, and his interaction with her was sometimes draining.

July 8, 1977 – I am very sad and exhausted. This is partly because of how long I have been traveling, but I don't think that's the only reason. I'm also sad and discouraged and that takes a lot of energy out of you. I seem so useless, and life seems to be so futile all the time. I don't know whether the big investment in M is either worth it or furthermore whether I really want to make it. I really don't know what I want. I've never been more confused, tired, and bored in my entire life.

After he returned home, this ambivalence continued.

August 9, 1977

What am I sick with?

A broken heart.

Why is my heart broken?

I've lost touch with real life. I've gone crazy.

Why have I gone crazy?

I don't know.

Age perhaps, maybe it's natural, maybe because of excessive pressure.

When did the break come?

First signs and intimations last spring. Dating, then with Billy's death a moroseness overcame me. I don't believe it has left. Later days included gradual craziness brought on by Germany and sightseeing.

November 29, 1977 – I still need to decide what I'm going to do with M. This has been so difficult to figure out that I have perpetually shelved the question to save myself undue trouble. I don't like the situation I find myself in. I am completely hemmed in, so to speak. On the one hand I do like, even love the girl, but on the other hand I'm not sure if anything can ever work out between us. (Dave was a believer in Christ and she was not.) I'm not sure she is really the girl for me. I'm not sure she's my type. I also don't know where I'd be without her—it could get very weird, and I don't know how to start all over without her. Sometimes it seems like the only thing to really do in the situation. But then I'm not sure it would be any different the next time around. So there is the inclination to try to keep the love I now have alive and to hope in it, or to step out into an uncertain situation. This is of course melodramatic. But then that's the kind of way my life has been. I wish I could start all over sometimes.

Finally, the crisis came. He broke up with his college girlfriend.

December 5, 1977 – I just lost my girlfriend, in effect. She was about all I had. I had to let her go. She treats me so badly and love isn't all it's cracked up to be at times. She could be very nice but that seemed to be infrequent with me. At least not frequent enough. I shouldn't have tolerated her for anywhere near the length of time that I tolerated her. It does something for me to finally get that fact into writing. I must have had masochistic tendencies.

As a new year began, Dave seemed on the verge of despair.

January 31, 1978 – I have broken up with M. It's been very difficult for me. I'm on my own now in a more radical way. At the risk of being melodramatic, that hasn't been easy. The emptiness is real, is very much there. I've never felt quite so alone and bereft of comfort and hope. I don't know whether it is related to this or not but I have felt considerably more crazy these past few days, especially in pressured situations. I feel like I am losing it more easily despite my desire to fight it off. This concerns me. Have also been quite sick for the last two weeks, a constant source of irritation and fatigue, especially if I am depressed.

Looking back later on this turmoil, he wondered with foreboding what would happen next.

When will all this end? I could be calculating and say it can only be resolved in one of three ways, none of which I am happy with. I will either continue to live sadly in my present state, or I will become part of the real world, or I will commit suicide. I hope that these are not the only three options, but they might be. My remaining hope is in a miracle from God. I don't know if it will happen. I do know this is an accurate chronicle of my inner mental anguish and torment.

Dave had begun to look for work near home, and got a factory job at a local furniture company. He had first sought an office position. His journal entries about this follow.

September 6, 1977 – No office job (available now). But I do have an opening on the second shift in the finishing department, in the factory. "Are you interested?" "Yes, I'll take it." I wonder how long I'm going to be with the factory. I wonder how much it matters. Nevertheless, I am upset about not getting the office job. I was pretty set on it, and I thought I would.

September 7, 1977 – Gloom over my fate as a factory worker continues to mount. A very boring day at the factory; no breaks, no special occasions. An absence of any sense of festivity or celebration is very evident. Life is dull, routine, and unromantic, and I would add unsatisfying. This, despite efforts of the employers to make the working area more cheerful and better, it remains a whole world in itself which nature's beauty cannot penetrate, which indeed seems to seal one off permanently from nature.

Work can be bad—I didn't realize how bad it has the potential to be. I think I am going to need to learn to cope with it better in some way. I'm terribly bored by it all already, dreadfully bored, beyond my endurance.

When an office job eventually opened up, he was at first relieved, but in time found it difficult to function well.

March 31, 1978 – Last day of March. Vacant because of traveling. I hope my mind doesn't stay too much that way, especially today at work.

June 12, 1978 – Noticeable lack of being able to function today. I become very defensive too quickly, being afraid of my own desires. I'm shy. I breathe hard and pretend no one will ever notice.

Another trying day at work. When will something come of all this? Furthermore, will I get any work done here?

Soon the inevitable came. Dave was fired.

June 13, 1978 – Most expensive day of the year. Cost: good reputation with many associates at work. My job (30 days). Absence of weekly $200 pay checks to follow.

Upon counting the cost, is it worth it? I have pursued erotic, romantic adventures whenever I had the desire. If in a day I want to be for real, something more than a rip-off, can I be believed? Can I say that I want to be a real man?

Can I be a real man? I think so. I'm so crazy, mixed up. An extravagant day working on the great cost reduction in the sky. I'm not working there much longer. A break will be good.

The best is yet to come. Further on down the road. So I've been knocked flat off my feet. No sense of crying about it now.

When Dave had to leave that job, his world began to fall apart. We, his parents, were visiting in the Soviet Union that summer with our Words of Hope Russian language broadcaster. We were never allowed to make phone calls back to the States. In those days the "Cold War" was frigid. We never felt welcome in the Soviet Union, except when we were in the churches. We didn't know what was happening in Dave's life. He couldn't continue to live in the rented home he had shared with a friend, so he moved back to Holland and stayed in our basement while we were away. As far as we could later ascertain, he did almost nothing there. He didn't even write in his journal.

When we arrived at home, we were concerned about him. We urged him to look for employment, but he seemed reluctant.

It appeared to us that he was simply vegetating at home. We didn't know what to do. A psychologist friend of ours urged us to give him a choice—either find work or live elsewhere.

Having at the time such scant awareness of the depth of Dave's struggle, we gave him that choice. He made a couple of attempts to find work, but to no avail. He went to stay with friends in Ann Arbor, but nothing opened up there. He finally decided to move to the old family home in Georgia to live with his grandparents. He would stay with them for a time, he said, hoping that something might turn up there. Our parents were uncertain about the wisdom of this, but consented to have him come.

We were heavy-hearted as he drove out of our driveway, uneasy about his future. We would later regret deeply what we had done. Moving to Georgia was no solution for Dave. He deteriorated rapidly. The grandparents did all they could to encourage him, but felt helpless as his condition worsened. Not in good health themselves, they became desperate.

What could be done? Our brother-in-law George Nickels, a psychologist living in Tallahassee, Florida, married to Helen's sister Janet, offered to take Dave into their home for a while and seek help for him in a nearby clinic. Dave went along. We talked with him by phone soon after he arrived there. He seemed friendly, but quite subdued, his voice faint.

11

Lost and Found!

That night, while the family slept, Dave drove off in his car, leaving no message. The next morning, George called to tell us, filled with self-accusation that he hadn't realized how ill Dave really was.

We were stunned, heartsick. It was the saddest time we had ever experienced. For two and a half days, Dave was missing. When no word came for long hours, Bill wrote this letter to him wherever he was, during a long night of sleeplessness:

November 12, 1978

Dear Dave,

I'm sitting here in my study at about 1:00 in the morning. I was in bed for a little while, but I woke thinking of you. I decided I'd get up and write to you. I'd like somehow to put into words some of what I'm feeling.

It's been almost 48 hours now since you left the Nickels' home in Tallahassee. We learned later Friday morning that you were gone. We've had no news of you since. It's been hard, Dave. Desperately hard. I feel terribly anxious and afraid. I don't know where you are or what has happened

to you. And when I think of how depressed you have been recently, my heart sinks within me. And one of my greatest fears is that you may have felt you had nowhere to go. You may have thought that we didn't want you here at home. You may not have known how much we love you.

Let me tell you, Dave, about how much you have been in my heart. I remember when you were born. You had a bright red birthmark on your forehead. I was frightened by that at first, but the doctor assured me it would fade, and it did. You were a chubby little baby—not very beautiful but marvelously winsome. You were stocky and strong.

I remember how you used to wrestle with Billy. He was a year and half older, taller and stronger. He could throw you, though you put up a real struggle. You seemed so frustrated at that, but you'd keep getting up and trying again.

I remember how you seemed to be a natural baseball player even when you were very young. You swung the wiffle-bat with a smooth, level, powerful swing. It wasn't long before you could throw a ball as far or farther than Billy could.

You were so conscientious. Once I found you underneath the front porch. You had taken a few pennies to buy some candy, and were eating it there secretly, and were mortified to be discovered.

It hurt you deeply when Billy became so sick. He had been your leader and buddy. You were anxious and afraid. You asked us, with evident pain, "Is Billy going to die?" It was hard for you to understand and accept what had happened to him. When he finally came home from the hospital, you were ecstatic. You wanted him to come out and play ball, just like you used to do together. But he couldn't manage it any more, and he quickly lost interest.

It was hard for you when he acted so differently. You couldn't communicate with him. He would sometimes hit or trip you and Jim, and he wasn't much fun to be around.

On the beach with baby Billy.

Baby Billy — play ball!

Look what got put in the basket! Billy and Dave.

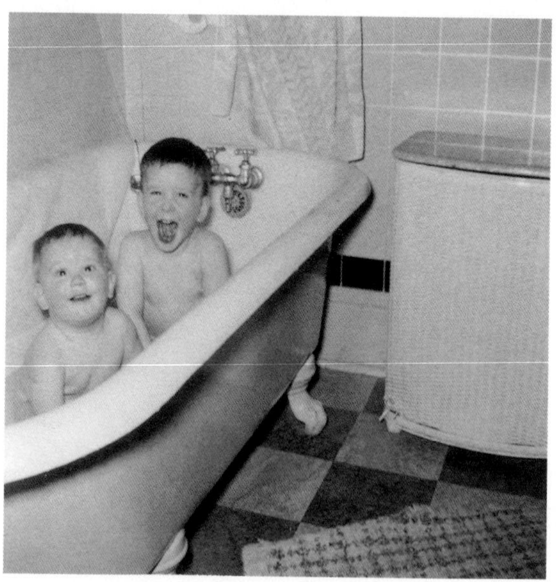

Billy and Dave love the tub.

Billy and Dave present brother Jim.

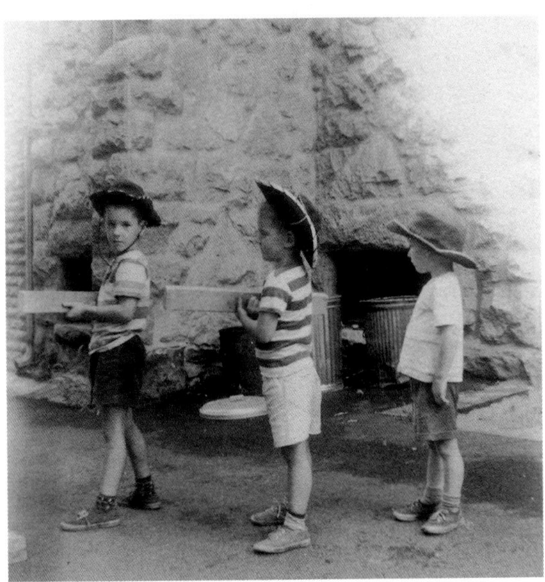

Playing soldiers (Billy leads Dave and Jim).

Enter baby Jonny. Now we're all here. What a tribe!

Out of the hospital! (Billy with the brace on his leg.)

Christmas in Chicago

Billy in back.
Jim, Jonathan, and Dave.

Christmas in Michigan

Jim, Billy, and Dave in back.
Jonathan, Helen, and Bill.

Surprise for Mom's and Dad's 25th Anniversary — a picture from the boys in which they all get dressed up in Dad's jackets. Our last picture of all four boys.

Dave with that warm and welcoming smile.

Dave and his golfing buddies: Paul, Jim, and Dad.

Dave's golf memorial picture.

The family home in Alamo, Georgia.
Now a funeral home near where Billy and Dave are buried.

Brownson Family Picture — Summer of 2005

Benjamin, Bill, Rachel, and Will (standing).
Sam, Jonathan, Jenny, Helen, and Jim (kneeling).
Joanna, Kathy, and Anna (seated).

I think of you in the house we moved into in Chicago. I can see you running around the circuit beginning in the living room—into the dining room, the kitchen, the back hall, my study, the front hall, and back to the couch again. You came sliding in, like it was second base.

Remember the day you were running through the house and slammed the plate glass living room door? It made a horrendous crash. We hardly dared look to see what had happened. That thick glass was in a million jagged pieces on the floor, and you were nowhere to be found. You had gone into hiding from the storm!

How you loved baseball! You played it with a wiffle ball or big softball in that tiny back yard on Wabash. Every now and then I'd take a bunch of you guys in the neighborhood out to Fernwood Park for a softball game. You wanted to play well—wanted it so much that you were frustrated and ornery if you didn't succeed. You played on the church team as a pitcher the last spring. We were in Chicago, and you were a budding star. You got a trophy for being on that team. We still have that in Billy's old room.

Remember Hightstown? You had a great time during those summers there. We had some happy ball games and batting practices. You liked the evening drives through the old abandoned war plant, when we scared up rabbits and pheasants.

We were there during the Cuban missile crisis. You heard the news about it, and were badly frightened. You looked at us with wide, pained eyes, "Are the Russians gonna bomb us?" We tried to reassure you, but we could tell you were upset.

Sometimes Billy's problems back in Chicago made your life difficult. You used to walk to and from school with him, and you were worried at what he might do. Embarrassed, too. It frustrated you that he was so unpredictable, and you felt responsible.

When he went away to Cove School, it took a lot of pressure off you and the other boys. You missed him, prayed for him, but life was much more relaxed for you when he was away.

You were happy about the move to Holland, but it was tough for you at first to break into the gang at school.

When you first tried to play on that fifth-grade basketball team you were barely second string, smaller than most of the others. But you had talent, and by the end of that year you were almost in the starting lineup. The next year you really began to develop as a dribbler and play-maker. You and Steve were a hot pair of sixth-grade guards.

You really loved your teacher. He would practice with you guys, or let you use the gym. He was a strong, caring man—a kind of a hero to you.

Your teachers sometimes thought you were fresh, but they liked you, and saw that you had a lot of potential. One of them especially was hard on you, but she thought you were great.

Junior high was a new thing—a longer way from home, a big, ugly building. You did well there in basketball. I remember scores of afternoons when I left the seminary early to see a game at the junior high school. I'd be excited all day on the day of a game. Watching you play was a high point in my week. I was jubilant when you did well, and I shared your disappointment—probably felt it even more than you did—on the bad days.

Then there was your baseball career. You were quite a pitcher in Little League days, but you grew very fast in junior high and developed arm problems. I can see you now with that green sling on your pitching arm while you were recuperating. That was tough.

There were some things about junior high that were not pleasant for you. I'll never forget that day when two bigger kids beat you up. You didn't know why they were picking on you, but they told you it was because your brother was a "mental." When Mom picked you up in the principal's office after that, you were almost hysterical. We went in your bedroom with you to try to give some comfort. The whole experience was so painful for you that you seemed inconsolable. [I just thought I heard the kitchen door open. I went out to check, and looked out the front windows to see if your car might be there, but it wasn't.] You pounded your head on the pillow and cried out in real anguish, "I could never believe in a God who would let that happen to my brother!"

That was the first time I remember that you expressed problems with the Christian faith. When we drove out to New York one summer, you aired a lot of your problems with accepting these things about God. You weren't at all sure about the whole business. That troubled me, but I was able to keep relatively quiet so that you could come out with the whole works. I felt good about that, and glad that you could open up in that way.

From then on through high school, though, you always seemed to hold yourself apart from the family faith. You were a good son—warm, loyal, affectionate, communicating a lot with us—but we felt that you weren't buying the gospel. It wasn't flagrant, open rejection, but we knew that you had your own thoughts.

You became interested during high school days in Zen Buddhism, and you pored over the works of Hermann Hesse. We felt at times that you were in a different world. We sometimes couldn't understand what you were talking about in "centering" and "feeling at one with everything."

I'm going to stop here for now, Dave, and go back to bed. Maybe I'll be able to sleep now. It helps to write these things out, because I can't talk to you, or even send you a letter. Dave, I don't know whether you're alive or dead, and it's the saddest, saddest experience of my whole life. I hope I'll wake up tomorrow to a new day, and that there will be good news that you are all right, and we'll learn where you are. But what will we do if no news comes? Or how will we stand it if they find your car somewhere but not you? Or if we learn that your beautiful life has somehow been snuffed out?

I'm hanging somewhere in space tonight, not knowing where I am or what's ahead. Waves of hurt and grief come washing over me. I think of where you might be, and the thoughts weigh me down. I remember how weak your voice was when we talked to you the night you left Nickels. It took you a long time to respond to each thing we said. You seemed warm and kind, but faint and far away. You told us you loved us a lot, and asked how we were doing. We told you a little bit, and then you asked the same question again. All of us seemed to run out of things to say.

Uncle George and Aunt Janet told us that you didn't even put on your shoes when you got up sometime early in the morning and drove away in your car. Where did you go, Dave? I wonder how far you could have gotten when you seemed to be so feeble and confused. What happened to you? Did you just get up by impulse and go out for some fresh air? If you planned to go a considerable distance, why did you leave everything you had there at Nickels' house? Those are the agonizing questions that torment me. It seems that by now you should have surely gotten oriented again. Even if you had taken some kind of drug in your depression and anxiety, the effects should have worn off by now. If you're well and reasonably alert, why don't we hear from you? You've always been one to call. You're so sensitive to what would worry or hurt us—it's not like you just to go off without letting us know something.

Did you go to some bar or nightspot and get in with some shady people? Did they beat you up and take your money, or worse than that? Did someone spot you where you parked and mug you and steal your car?

Or did you have drugs with you and take too much, so that you're lying somewhere, out of it? These questions probably sound foolish—maybe it's also unwarranted. Maybe you're resting well somewhere and we'll hear from you soon. But the questions keep coming.

Now I'll ask that hardest one of all, Dave. Were you so discouraged about things, so crushed that life has been falling apart for you that it no longer seemed worth it to live? Did you come to the conclusion there in Tallahassee that there was nothing left for you and you wanted to escape?

Oh, Dave, how can I tell you what those thoughts do to me? That you should be so unhappy is heartrending to me. I don't know why, don't begin to know why you've had so much inner pain. But I feel it with you—so much. I try to put myself in your place as I reflect on things.

I hear from the folks in Georgia that a letter you had been writing to us says that "the noose is tightening," and my blood runs cold. But I remember. After graduation (and long before it) you were deeply troubled because you didn't know what to do. You felt that the things you wanted to do—be a writer, be creative and artistic—you lacked the talent to do. Nothing opened up for you in the community. You took a job that seemed good at first, but it wasn't what you wanted. You didn't give yourself wholly to it, and so you had to leave. That was shattering.

The relationship with M had some good things in it, but didn't seem to work out. You began to have those withering doubts about your identity as a man.

You came home to live, tried to get yourself together, took a job for two days, but found that you couldn't handle the relationships there. We felt it wasn't good for you to be sitting around in the house all day idle, so we pressured you to get a job or live elsewhere. You moved down to Ann Arbor, thinking to pick up your Christian life there again. You were in the house with Rob, and the brothers treated you well, but getting back into that community life was too different, too much.

You wanted to come back home, but we said you couldn't without a definite plan. You decided to go to Georgia. We wanted you to make the arrangements for yourself. You did, and came home for a few days. We wondered when you would leave for Georgia—you seemed to be dragging your feet. We urged you to get moving and after about six days you left, planning to spend a night in Ann Arbor on the way south.

Did you feel then, Dave, that we were forcing you out when you felt you needed to stay? Were you asking for help, waiting for us to take initiative for you to be hospitalized and get counseling? Did we blow it then—completely and tragically? Did we send you away when you most needed us—send you to a situation that had no real possibilities of help for you, to a place where both you and the folks would only grow more anxious?

That's what haunts me, Dave. I don't know what to say. I was impatient when you slept away your days and did nothing. I felt you were going downhill at home. But I was foolish to think that it would be better in Georgia. I thought I was treating you like an adult, insisting that you assume responsibility, but now my way of handling it seems so desperately wrong. Forgive me, Dave. Wherever you are, please forgive me. Believe me, if you can, when I say that I would never, in a thousand lifetimes, have sent you away had I known how things would go in Alamo. It crushes me to think that my misguided urgings made up part of that noose that tightened around you.

Oh, Dave, I don't know what went wrong. Mom and I have loved you so much! Not always wisely, I know. But our prayers have risen for you, and our hearts have gone out to you times without number. I really believe that if there were anything I could possibly have done to make you truly happy, I would have done it. Your joys have been our joys and your

pain ours as well. Somehow our concern for you wasn't helpful, and it was hard for you to accept your lot in our family and faith. Oh, I wish we had done better, and that life could have been more relaxed and happy for you! Maybe my intensity about the faith and about life brought too much strain to you. All I can say, Dave, is that I love you, and want more than words can say that you should find fulfillment and joy in your life with the Lord, and that somehow the doubts about yourself, the fears and conflicts that have plagued you might be swept away forever.

I've lived a full life, Dave. If God should take me at any time, I would feel that it had been great to live, and that God had given me more than any man could rightly hope for. But you're only 24. And there's so much potential yet untapped in you, so much promise unfulfilled. Oh, Dave, please live! Please say yes to who you are and what you've received. Please stay with us—don't leave us behind. Such a big part of us goes when you go, and God's world loses so very much. Wherever you are, whatever has become of you, please, please come home. The light in the driveway is on. We're keeping the kitchen door open all night. Please come.

Love, Dad

Weeping endured for two nights, but joy came at morning, as Bill writes:

November 14, 1978
Praise God! Praise God! The good news came on that "new day"—Sunday, the Lord's day. Dave was found in Montgomery, Alabama. He had fallen off a bridge, about 15 feet high, and was taken to a hospital in Montgomery. The troopers had received the bulletin from the Holland police and called us about 4:40 Sunday afternoon.

Helen relives that moment:

My heart leaped. I urged the trooper not to let him go, and hurriedly hung up so we could make calls. Bill called our sons while I agreed to run next door and use another phone to call a doctor. As I left the house, my feet hardly touched the ground. I leaped and shouted, "He's alive! He's alive!!" Then I thought of the prodigal son's father—always watching for him and looking for him to come home. *How could anyone not rejoice,* I thought. "This our son was dead and he's alive." What a joy! We didn't know what might lie ahead, but we felt we could endure anything since our Dave was alive.

From Bill

We arrived in Montgomery about 6:40 Monday morning, and reached the hospital soon after. There he was, scraggly beard, cuts and bruises all over his face, lying on a hospital bed with his eyes closed—the most beautiful sight we had ever beheld!

We wonder if we'll ever find out what happened in those two and a half days. Dave's car was found abandoned on I-85, south of Montgomery. He had apparently been trampling through the woods without shoes on, as his feet and ankles were covered with scratches. He was found by patrolmen after someone reported to them that they had seen him sitting on the edge of a bridge and then falling backward over the side. He fell some 15 feet to the ground beneath.

When the officers found him lying there, they asked him questions. At first he was unresponsive, but later he told them his name and address. State troopers had received the missing person alert from the Holland police and realized that this was he. Just as he was being transferred to St. Margaret's Hospital in Montgomery, they were calling us.

No broken bones, vital signs good—praise God for his gracious protection! Dave spoke very little yesterday, although at times something of his personality came through. Some confusion in his thinking, sometimes blankness in his eyes. When the nurses were asking him some routine questions, they came to the matter of when he usually goes to bed. A pause, then a chuckle, "Not very early lately!"

We called from Montgomery to our long-time friend, Dr. Truman Esau, psychiatrist and chief of staff at Old Orchard Psychiatric Hospital in Skokie, Illinois. He encouraged us to bring Dave there.

When we were admitting him on Monday evening, he was slow in responding to some questions. Occasionally we answered for him. Question by the lady at the desk: "Religion?" I responded quickly, "Protestant." Dave corrected me: "It's Christian, not Protestant!"

As we were in the treatment room on the fourth floor of the hospital, staff members were asking Dave questions about how he came to be there. Dave was articulate at times, answering questions intelligently, but some responses were hard to understand.

When Dave had settled in at Old Orchard Hospital, Dr. Esau sat down with him and introduced himself as a friend of his parents. Would that matter to Dave? Dave shook his head. He didn't mind. Then he spoke the words he had spoken first when in the Alabama hospital: "I'm taking the long road home." He also indicated that he would be willing to go on medication to quiet the voices he was hearing and to relieve him of oppressive thoughts.

We left him at the Old Orchard Hospital and flew home, not aware then of the long, long road it would be for him and for us!

12

First Hospitalization

Dave remained in the psychiatric hospital for several weeks. We drove down periodically to become involved in his therapy. The doctor had made the shocking discovery that Dave believed himself guilty for his brother Billy's illness at age six, and also for his subsequent death. In their childhood wrestling on the bed one night, Billy had fallen on the floor. Dave, as a five-year-old, had later believed that Billy's brain injury was his fault! He had lived with that dark dread from early childhood. And we never understood that. It was heartbreaking to think about what Dave had carried within him all those years, and that we didn't know how to help him.

Dr. Esau used sodium amytal to help Dave recover these childhood memories. He taped their conversation. Here is part of what Dave recalled:

That illness really hurt us a lot. It hurt when he came back from the hospital. He wanted to be the big cheese but he was sick and couldn't do it. We acted like he was the same but then after awhile he hurt people and threw things. We stuck with him more as a leader but he couldn't do it and was mad. It was so sad when he couldn't walk. All the happiness wasn't there anymore. I never tried to compete with him then. Billy couldn't walk. He was my big brother and my happiness. I didn't care about my happiness because my brother couldn't walk. Billy was more important than I was. He was always more important than I was. (How does a little boy get happy again?) He can't be happy. You don't know how hard it was when your brother couldn't walk. He was a different person. I couldn't communicate with him. You don't understand. He always wanted to walk and run and he couldn't run anymore. A little boy can't get happy again when his brother can't walk. You don't understand. I think he ran too hard.

He ran too hard and got sick. My dad was broken in two. Do you see how unhappy my dad is? Billy was the best brother there ever was. Weren't we unhappy when he went away, Dad? We were so sad we couldn't stand it. [Dave is wailing at this point.]

(What's going to happen to Dave?) It doesn't matter. I want to stay back with Billy. I felt so bad for so long. He was so much better and so much more fun than anyone else was. More daring. He'd do anything and I lost him. They had to take him to a hospital and I didn't know what a hospital was.

Mom and Dad were nice then. They were the type of people that wouldn't bother anyone else. It was neat to be a part of the family. They liked to do things like help people. We played games. Dad and I had intense competition going on. Those were really neat times. There were no bad times. It was an ideal childhood till Billy was sick. I was having too much fun. Billy always had these programs to do. It was really a nice bygone era. We moved and everything was cold.

After his early sessions with Dave, Dr. Esau recorded these insights:

November 18, 1978

Acute schizophrenic episodes are marked by delusions and hallucinations.

There is a lack of correlation between what one feels and thinks.

Everything feels flat and grey.

Pain is so great you cease to feel.

Support is needed and someone to help one find the truth.
The way out is the warmth of human beings who care.
Insight is needed about distortions and there is a need to recognize that others see relatively better.
We process to bring feelings back and they must be appropriate.
This can happen quickly.
Nothing needs to be chronic.
Dave was like twins—his perceptions of himself like Billy. It's like losing a parent.

When Dave later left the hospital, he wrote the following analysis of his treatment:

The therapy has helped me reach certain specific goals in terms of reintegration into the family. On the other hand persistent problems remain. It may be partly because I can't seem to believe in myself. I want to get somewhere and I don't know how or where.

Long-term problems:

- hallucinations—voices
- fantasy of being "on the air"
- unusual pains
- feeling of being judged
- religiously failing
- manipulative
- negative self-image
- basic shyness
- last two years, feeling of utter helplessness in the face of things
- physical alterations; inability to take medicines perhaps due to some damage in my physical system
- A psychotic identity
- A certain perception of a cognitive split between myself and those around me (a feeling of rejection)
- Restless, uneasy, unhappy. Do I expect this, do I expect anything else? I went to the psychotic world for some kind of a

change but didn't anticipate the horrible problems that could develop. I don't concretely know what I want now and where my feelings are, and I find it hard to believe in myself that I can change and find life to be more meaningful and rewarding. I also find it hard to be in the "now" in terms of relationships, as I constantly am either reverting to the past (studying comparative identity) or feeling it difficult to deal with a pretty constant mixture of feelings that leave me pretty raw and on edge. But I keep hoping that somehow I will be able to have and experience feelings with others that build a sense of belonging.

December 27, 1978 – I feel a need to establish some basic goals for my therapy, and for my life as well.

- I want to improve in relating to other people, both men and women.
- I want to slowly grow in being comfortable socially, enough to be able to leave the hospital.
- I want to exercise every day, and get back into shape physically.
- I want to plan out my future as much as possible.
- I want to deal with problems that come up directly, and try to improve on being passive in the face of my fears about my own personality.
- I want to remain young at heart, able to live freely with those younger, older, and at the same age.
- I want to settle down one day and marry.

It was Christmas time when Dave came home from the hospital. We hung a huge "Welcome Home—Dave!" banner in our living room. We cherished hopes that the nightmare of his illness was ending. He seemed reasonably calm and self-controlled. He entered into the joy of our Christmas celebration.

But Dave wasn't certain about what should come next. He felt lonely and lacking in confidence. He lived with us at the family home and began to see some of his old friends. He enrolled at Western Theological Seminary in Holland and took a course or two.

As time went on, he became more troubled and restless. He felt a need for further hospitalization, so we arranged for him to be admitted again to Old Orchard Hospital in Skokie, Illinois, under the care of Dr. Esau.

It was then that we realized more and more the depth and tenacity of his mental illness. Dr. Esau described it as a "schizo-affective disorder." Dave heard voices, experienced hallucinations, had delusions of grandeur. He experienced mood-swings of a bi-polar kind—manic highs followed by times of exhaustion and depression. But he didn't have the difficulty in relationships that many schizophrenics experience. He was capable of warm, strong friendships. What he was to do with the rest of his life remained a source of acute anxiety.

When Dave's brothers heard about his second hospitalization, they were heartsick. They realized then that Dave's illness was to be serious and enduring. Jim told us how he went into the sanctuary of the church he was serving and paced up and down, deep in sadness, boiling with anger. Could this happen again to a God-fearing family, leaving another brother so stricken? How could God allow it? Faith was shaken, sorely tested. But after long wrestling, he knew there was nowhere else to turn. "Lord, to whom shall we go?"

13

On the Roller Coaster

We, as parents, experienced the same dismay. As in the following months one hospitalization for Dave followed another, we felt ourselves on an emotional roller coaster. Dave would make progress, it seemed, and then return home. Our hopes for his full recovery would revive. But again and again he would return to his psychotic world and need to be hospitalized. As time went on, we became almost afraid to hope—the disappointments were too devastating.

It's painful how, in situations like this, parental expectations for children begin to shrink. At first, we had hoped for Dave's full recovery and return to normal life. After several hospitalizations, we began to wonder if he could ever hold a regular job or be able to marry. Then, as we realized more and more the depths of his inner anguish, we began to question the possibility that he could ever know real peace again. We can remember days when our expectations were reduced to this: "Oh, if Dave could only live one day free from his inner torment!"

Here are some of Bill's journal entries that trace our highs and lows through those years:

February 17, 1979 – I praise you, Lord, for the wonderful work of restoration in Dave. Now in his time of loneliness and uncertainty about the future, please encourage his heart. Move him to look toward you, to hope in you. Be his portion and his strength.

August 25, 1980 – Dave has had a tough time these last few days. That was a part of my heaviness this morning. He went to a bachelor party Saturday night. A bad set-back. We had some talk and prayer together yesterday which seemed to help, but today was another hard day there at the foster-care facility where Dave worked. A pastor friend went over with Helen to talk to Dave tonight. Was a real help. What a caring, supportive counselor he has been!

September 25, 1980 – I hardly know where to start. Dave has been enrolled at seminary, attending classes for two weeks. It has been a tense, heavy time. His fears of annihilation persist. He's convinced that he has blown it terribly and that now there is no hope for him. Seems troubled almost incessantly with tormenting voices. He is extremely passive, finds it difficult to get out of bed in the morning, almost impossible to do concentrated study. He has missed classes, slept through responsibilities, and manifested difficulty in managing his life. Helen and I have been giving a great deal of time and energy just trying to support him and keep him going. We feel often discouraged, drained, at a loss.

Tonight we talked with Dave about the decisions before us. He has difficulty accepting the thoughts we shared about his identification with Billy, his finding it hard to rise above his childhood model. When asked his understanding of the situation, he responded with conviction (1) That he has badly screwed up his life, and (2) That now there is no hope of changing it. We talked about options—move to the seminary lodging or possibly another hospitalization. Dave didn't know what he wanted.

We talked to Dr. Esau. Dave acknowledged his passivity, feeling of helplessness. Dr. Esau outlined possibilities for long-term hospitalization. Suggested that to pull out of seminary might be worth trying. Perhaps this was too soon, or a wrong direction. See if the better condition of this past summer returns. Dave had no conviction about what would be best. Said maybe he needed to be hospitalized. We went to bed, but I couldn't sleep.

Can it be that Dave is so sick that he can't recover, so damaged that the wound can't be healed? That has been the deep underlying fear that I've kept fighting back. It seems at least that some form of long-term hospital care may be ahead. Will the bright potential of still another son be blighted? Will Dave drift further into an inner world, away from relationships and responsibility? Is adulthood and a demanding world just too painful and threatening for him to face? O, Lord, don't let that happen! Let him truly live! Let him be happy and fulfilled! Let him know who he is, and give him the inner strength to come home again!

We feel spent, Lord. So much pain and sadness, so much frustration that all our words and prayers, love and effort can't seem to help him! We know we can't go on like this, especially when I'll need to be away a good deal in the next two months. But to see him go away is almost like losing another son. What will it do to him, to us? To Jim and Kathy, Jon and Jenny?

What are you doing in all this, Lord? Where are you? You know our pain; you know what Dave is suffering. You know how much we long to see him whole. Talk about "good gifts," Father! You are the one who gives them. But somehow the good gift of healing never came to Billy in this life, and inner healing doesn't seem to come for Dave either. I know you love us; I know you're there, but this seems so terribly sad. Your touch can heal, Lord Jesus, but our son is so sick, and we seem to cry out to you in vain. Why, Lord? I feel so at a loss, so weak in faith, so weary in spirit. My stomach churns; my heart is dull; I'm in great heaviness. Lord, how long?

I don't understand your ways. To accept the crippling of two beautiful sons seems too much. It's the closest I've been in my sheltered life to Gethsemane. Please take this bitter cup away, Lord. I want to keep on struggling to see my son healthy, giving himself to your service. For what are all the struggles, prayers, and tears if he is to decline and vegetate? How will that praise you? How can that serve your purpose? I don't want it, Lord! Everything in me cries out against his spending the rest of his life mentally ill. Why should it have to be? I don't want to believe it has to be that way. I don't want to give up hoping for Dave, don't want to lose him.

But, Lord, if there's no other way, no other way but this heartbreak, this tragedy, if somehow this suffering has to be, if your loving purpose somehow works through it, if in your wonderful fatherly kindness you see it must be, then let your will be done. I give Dave over into your hands. He's yours. I can't hold on to him. I can't seem to help him. I know you love him much more than I ever could. And one day, like Billy, he'll be completely well. Guard him, Lord, from all evil until that day.

October 29, 1980 – Dave is hanging on at seminary. He gets to most classes, does some assignments, but is troubled with fears and self-doubts a good bit of the time. The weary struggle continues. He's managing to function, but it's hard to see that he's making much progress. Lord, I believe; help my unbelief.

And please, Lord, help Dave to deal with those painful feelings that lead him to choose the voices. Help him to learn to accept your forgiveness, to accept his human-ness, his limitations. Help him to build new patterns of thought, new ways of dealing directly with his feelings. It seems like such a huge mountain to get over, such a labyrinth to find his way through. Let there be some fresh glimmers of light this week.

Then, a turn for the better. Glimmers of light began to come.

December 11, 1980 – What a difference a few weeks can make! When I read back over what it was like with Dave in September and October, it's like reliving a bad dream. Since Dave finished his first quarter at Western, things have been *so much better.*

That quarter was a real struggle. It seemed at times that he was barely hanging on, and we felt like we were expending lots of time and vital energy to pull him through his exams and final assignments. I helped him get ready for tests; Helen typed papers while he dictated.

He was frequently frustrated, intensely fearful, but seemed to have some underlying determination to make it.

After he finished his last exam there was profound relief—for him and for us. That week (Thanksgiving) was a relaxed one for us all—good interaction with family and friends. Then that Saturday at his decision he moved to seminary housing. As we look back on it now, that seems a momentous step.

It's been almost two weeks since he moved there. The change from last quarter has been marked—thrilling, in fact. He has been getting to classes, even at 8:00 a.m.! Good interaction with Jeff, Keith, and Jim, some of the guys he's living with. His colloquy of five students has had an excellent sharing time, with prayer and singing. Dave's participation in that was so rich that one friend called me up excitedly the other night to tell me about it.

We haven't seen Dave since Sunday. At nights he's been studying, exercising, or involved in seminary functions. He seems to be applying himself to Hebrew and church history—getting down to studying better than at any time in recent years.

Helen and I look at each other here at home with broad smiles, shake our heads in wonder, weep tears of joy. Dave has found a place to be, a community of which he's a part. He's moving toward adulthood, toward vocation. He's still troubled at times by the self-tormenting inner voices, by painful feelings of how he has blown it, but there is more and more functioning and progress in spite of those things. He's on the way! The real Dave, an extraordinary, beautiful person is emerging more and more. Praise God!

It's a delicious feeling that he is functioning well, getting along—without our feverish efforts! When he calls on the phone the feelings are warm, but he doesn't seem dependent on us. It seems that some deep family bonding has happened, and now he's able to move out on his own into the world of relationships and responsibility. Not all the way yet, but noticeably, genuinely. Joy!

By the fall of 1981, our joy was fading, and the old sadness returned.

September 18, 1981 – Dave had a very bad day. He experienced thickness of tongue, inability to control his mouth. He was afraid it was another psychotic experience coming on, feared he might need to be hospitalized. Had been walking around in an almost desperate state until found by a seminary friend, taken to see our pastor. Dr. Esau had been called, and we were not to leave until touching base with him tonight.

This hit me like a sledgehammer. We had been building our hopes again, seeing signs of healing and progress in Dave. I had moments when I let myself feel what it would be like to see him whole and happy again. Now this! It was like the old painful wound opened again. I felt suddenly old, spent, weary. Great heaviness, hard to fight back despair, hard even to feel like fighting it.

A call to Dr. Esau convinced us (and Dave) that those physical reactions were side-effects of Dave's starting again to use [a medication] heavily, and without the counterbalancing medicine. Felt much better about that, but much pain and self-reproach that my anger and impatience Wednesday night had made Dave feel again that he had nowhere to go with his feelings. How hard it is for me to learn, how hard to accept and listen patiently to Dave's negative feelings. I become so absorbed with how they affect me, so hurt and anxious that I seem unable to respond helpfully to him. Lord, help!

September 20, 1981 – Just before church another awkward, tense situation with Dave. Trivial disagreement over a certain play in a cribbage game. Instead of admitting freely my thoughtless, dumb play, I said that Dave was partly responsible. He reacted against that; I got more defensive. Finally as we sat outside church, I was helped to acknowledge my dumb play, poor handling of it. Tension eased, burden lifted for worship.

Dave has a hard time accepting those childish behaviors of mine in a parent. I have a hard time admitting them!

November 18, 1981 – Two weeks ago last Friday he went back into Old Orchard Hospital. We had gone down with him that afternoon for an appointment with Dr. Esau. Dave was clear in mind, but depressed and alienated. It became evident that the year at seminary was not working out for him, that dependence on us was making him increasingly hostile. He decided to enter the hospital, called his professor to explain. Wants to sort things out about where he should be, differentiate in some way from his family.

Dr. Esau began to explore with him the possibility of long-term hospitalization, a program of gradual rehabilitation. Dave showed interest in this, indicated a preference for the nearest one. Now it appears that that will be the next step.

As we were going to sleep tonight, Helen and I were reflecting about this, having mixed feelings. It seems like the only alternative at this point, but will it be simply a re-run of past hospitalizations? Will Dave recount his inner fears and agonies to a new set of listeners without moving in a new direction? I woke up shortly before 2:00, with these things on my mind. Couldn't sleep, felt like writing. As I've read over the entries in this journal since the Soviet Union trip, I feel oppressed, heavy, weak in hope. The night Dave went back in the hospital I went through a storm of grief, anger, crying out in pain and protest to God. Since then I've felt emotionally spent. What more is there to feel, to write, to pray, to do? The nightmare goes on.

How bleak and dark the future must look to Dave now! Four hospitalizations in the last three years, now facing another one—long-term. Couldn't stay with his job, couldn't get another job around home. Couldn't stay in Ann Arbor or Georgia. After being in the hospital: couldn't stay on at Words of Hope, couldn't keep functioning in seminary, couldn't find comfort even in relating to his own family, had difficulty sustaining relationships with others. Can't go on being dependent on his parents, but sees no sustaining alternatives. How will things get better? What can he look to that will kindle hope? He has feared utter disaster for a long time. Will he see this as one more proof that he's doomed, one more step toward condemnation?

And what about us? How can we look at this? When I think about what will go on at a new facility, I wonder if anyone or anything there can make a significant difference. I want to hope, want to see the possibilities in a gradual rehabilitation program, but it's hard to envision what the factors will be that can promote healing. I'm thrown back again, Lord, on your miracle-working power, your healing grace. That's my hope—I can't really see any other. Don't disappoint my hope!

The struggle goes on.

March 31, 1982 – My stomach is churning as I begin to write. I woke up at about 5:15 this morning and couldn't get back to sleep. On my mind—Dave.

He came home from Old Orchard Hospital nine days ago after a stay of almost five months. He didn't want either new facility. He didn't want to settle in Chicago or somewhere away from family, friends, familiar supports. He moved back to Holland with the intent of living in seminary housing until the end of the school year, looking for a job.

Through his oversight, ours, and the hospital's, it wasn't noted until the last two weeks that his hospitalization policy covers only 80% of the expenses. He owes the hospital something over $6,800. Yesterday he had to pay a bill for car repair of $430. But those things seem minor, almost trivial. A thousand anxious questions keep forcing themselves on us. Can Dave survive? Can he get and hold a steady job? Can he possibly live with any degree of independence? Can he make arrangements to eat adequately, to get up on time, to keep up his appearance, to get exercise, to manage his finances, care for his car? None of that seems clear right now.

It's desperately hard for him to sit at a meal in a restaurant, to go to church (last Sunday, he didn't make it in Traverse City when brother Jim was preaching), carry on a conversation. Monday night he sat with us watching the NCAA basketball finals, but hardly said a word, showed little emotional response. Yesterday I told him about my conversation with an official at his place of work, but three hours later he didn't seem to remember that, asked me if I was going to call him.

What can he do? Where can he go for help? Helen and I are planning to leave tomorrow for nine days in Georgia with Mary Alice [Bill's stepmother], J.V. and Dick [Bill's sister and brother-in-law]. We've planned that for a long time, feel the contacts with them are important. But uncertainty about how Dave can handle things while we're away hangs over us like a dark cloud. We know he has to learn to function on his own, to get some separateness from us (and we from him), but it's hard to envision what he will do with himself in these coming days.

Helen is feeling all this keenly. It's an awful lot to deal with. With Dave, the forces of darkness, disease, and despair almost seem too strong for you to scatter. Even as I write that it sounds ridiculous. I know it can't be true, but how else do we deal with what's happening in Dave's life? Was he damaged in early youth beyond repair—like losing an eye, a leg, or brain cells that never come back? Did he at some point choose the wrong way—irreversibly? Is it fruitless, then, even to pray for his healing in this life, as it seemed to be with Billy?

I know you love us, Lord, and I believe you love Dave. I'd rather think you can't help than that you don't care. But if this tragedy really can't change, then what meaning have all the prayers, clingings to hope, claimings of the promises, struggles and tears? I'm struggling, groping, sick inside.

Later that spring, Dave's situation seemed even more hopeless. Bill left for a ministry trip amid gathering gloom.

May 14, 1982 – Father, as I begin this trip I feel heavy-hearted. Dave's situation weighs on my spirit. His outbursts on Wednesday night were so vile and hostile that I felt numb, but now the pain of that is intense. He seems to be trying to destroy the close ties he still has, to cut himself off emotionally from us as a way of dying. He seems less committed than before to getting well, more resigned to living in his own inner world.

It's hard to know what's best for him now. If he stays long at Holland Hospital, he'll pile up a huge debt he cannot pay. If he comes home, he'll feel trapped in dependency and become hostile. The state hospital seems like a possibility, but we aren't sure he'll be willing to go, or that he can get in. And if he does go there, will he find help? He isn't willing to take any medication for fear of distressing side-effects. A state hospital will be sparsely staffed. Will he have enough significant interaction with others there to keep from vegetating? Or will he lapse more deeply and hopelessly into hearing inner voices?

We're running out of options. The gloomy view Dave has of his future seems to be proving true. It's hard to see anything at this point that can turn his situation around and start him on the road to recovery. It's becoming increasingly doubtful that he believes that can happen, or even deeply wants it to.

We're really up against it. If you don't intervene in some way this nightmare can only get worse. But you seem silent and far off. Our prayers, thus far, are unavailing. This malignant illness seems unchecked, the demonic powers in control. Is Dave right that he has been abandoned, that there is no hope for him? Are we fools to think that faith and prayer can affect psychosis?

It's terribly hard to accept this as your will. This inner misery, this terrible despair—you cannot want that for anyone. You are the Father of mercies. Dave's affliction benefits no one. It's wearing us all down. I see no way in which you are glorified in it—it seems to drive Dave into raging against you, hating you and others, despising himself.

Why, Lord? Why Billy and all his afflictions? Why Dave with far worse suffering? Why such chronic sorrow that seems to have no end? We groan, we cry out with pain, we grow old and weary, we have little heart for your service. Can this have any meaning, any value?

I hardly dare to ask for you to deliver Dave. I've asked so many times before and been disappointed. I've hoped over and over again, but seemingly in vain. Can it be that you're mocking me? Keeping me praying and hoping when it's all for nothing? I can't believe that. Surely you'll let me see the goodness of the Lord in the land of the living. You'll bring about some change; you'll show us some sign of healing and improvement in Dave. You've promised that you won't fail us or forsake us. Please don't fail us. Please don't leave us alone. Please don't abandon Dave. Don't let that precious life be lost in despair. Do something! Reveal yourself to him. Incline his heart toward you. Don't break the bruised reed or quench the smoking flax. Have mercy upon him, and upon us, for your name's sake. You are our only hope. Show yourself strong on our behalf. Arise for our help, O Lord!

Show us, I pray, anything that we are to do for Dave in these days. Give us light as to how we can best serve your purposes in his situation. And please help us not to get in the way! We're just about at the end of our rope. Will you do something for Dave and for us soon? Will you make us glad as many days as you have afflicted us, as many years as we have seen evil?

It all seems so impossible, Lord. I can't even visualize how your salvation might come to Dave. Gloriously surprise us, Father! Do for us in this affliction far above all we can ask or think.

14

The Long, Bumpy Road

From Bill

October 27, 1982 – How different everything seems as I begin to write! How marvelously the Lord has worked in Dave's situation!

On May 12, we had Dave admitted to Holland Hospital's psychiatric wing. That was one of the darkest days of our lives. Dave had not been doing well in his recent work at a turkey processing plant, breaking equipment, getting in minor forms of trouble. There was that arrest out in Port Sheldon where police found him on private property, trespassing. Dave took the whole matter hard. He had been causing some disturbance at his housing, sometimes screaming out in the night.

On that Wednesday, he came from work and began to act in bizarre ways—talking in a woman's voice, sitting in an upstairs window. We were called; Jon and I went there. Dave wouldn't go with us, spoke with contempt about the possibility of going home, shouted obscenities at me.

Son Jon went with him as he walked away. Later they came back and Dave consented to come home with us. Our pastor and a physician friend came over; Dave finally consented to have himself admitted. Before that I had gone on a long, wild walk with him in which he shouted blasphemies, screamed at passing cars.

His first days in Holland Hospital showed little progress. We were exploring the possibility of long-term hospitalization at a state hospital, but were told Dave couldn't be admitted unless definitely suicidal. Even if admitted, he would probably be soon released. No answer in that direction.

Dave resisted taking any anti-psychotic medications because he had experienced distressing side effects from some of them before. After a couple of weeks he finally consented to try a new medication.

The next day he was noticeably better, more communicative, less hyper, less troubled. Then began a long, gradual upgrade of progress which has continued until now. Dave came home after about ten weeks of hospitalization. He has been involved since in a partial hospitalization program 9:30–3:50 Monday, Wednesday, and Friday.

It's hard to express how much better he is. Everyone sees it in his face. The haunted, pained look is gone. His face in repose is calm and peaceful. And he smiles—freely and often!

Our relationship with him is the best it has ever been. He is warm, affectionate, thoughtful, and very appreciative. He relates to others with sensitivity and charm; he is very affirming to those in his small group at the hospital, and has formed a real friendship with a family nearby.

He's able to go to church again, remains attentive, and finds it enjoyable and helpful. He has been reading the Scriptures regularly for the first time in who knows when.

He talks about his depressed and anxious feelings with us, and seems to respond wonderfully well to our listening and encouragement. We feel that we are able to give him a good deal of support, which he is glad and grateful for.

He still isn't at all clear about vocational direction, and has anxieties about that. He would like to marry, but has doubts also about whether he'll be able to handle it. But he is feeling more comfortable with himself, his family, his faith, and where he is right now.

For us, it's like an immense burden lifted. The constant inner pain of years isn't there these days. Having Dave around is not tension, frustration and anguish, but a real joy. It's as though we're waking up from a long, terrible nightmare. Lord, how can we ever thank you?

January 2, 1983 – This has been a blessed holiday time for our family. Dave's progress has continued in a most heartening way. He has a part-time job at the Hope College bookstore, which has been for him a gradual, strengthening re-entry into the world of work. He hasn't smoked in about six weeks now, which has aided both his health and his self-confidence. Though with occasional spells of discouragement, he has kept on moving ahead, with a growing consciousness that he has already come a long way. Issues like marriage and vocational direction are still very uncertain for him, but he is dealing with that uncertainty in a better way, and often feels a measure of peace about where he is at the moment. One big concern of his for 1983—to lose weight around the middle and get in good physical condition.

Dave had a fine time relating to the rest of the family during the holidays. He got along well with Jeannette and Kathy and enjoyed [his nieces] Rachel and Anna greatly.

May 11, 1983 – Dave has mingled feelings, I'm sure. He's really happy for Jon and Jenny [in the birth of their son, Ben], but it reminds him again of what hasn't been possible for him, of the way his younger brothers seem many stages ahead of him now. He has his times of discouragement, when gloom settles in, but he keeps plugging away at his work (he has been full-time at the college bookstore for over a week now) and doesn't stay down.

June 23, 1983 – I woke up at about 2:00 a.m. today with many things on my mind, finally got up just before 3:00 to put down these thoughts:

Reading the entries back through November 18, 1981 reminds me of the marvelous, almost overwhelming changes in Dave's life. He is still doing splendidly. He is a thoughtful, affirming son to us—remarkably so. He has become more and more a caring friend to his brothers and their families. He seems to find a measure of joy and fulfillment in his work at the bookstore, even though the pay is low and the work sometimes rather menial. He is relating very positively toward those with whom he works.

He's in the best physical condition he has experienced in years—smoking gone, excess weight largely lost, regular in running and weightlifting, doing well in softball. He talks more and more confidently about eventual marriage, seems to look forward to that. He doesn't have very definite plans about his vocational future, but seems pretty much at peace about moving into that a day at a time. He bounces back quickly and strongly, we notice, from low moods.

September 5, 1983 – Dave continues to make good, gradual progress. He has weathered the initial strains of this new job as manager of the Hope College mail room, and finds his work at times to give him some fulfillment as well as structure.

November 11, 1983 – Dave continues to make progress, though with some setbacks and tough days. He keeps hanging in there. Lord, give him light about his vocational direction and make plain to him any steps he's to take toward marriage. Heal him fully, I pray. Let all his powers and gifts be released for effective ministry in your name.

But the releasing hadn't yet come fully. Other setbacks were still ahead.

January 24, 1984 – Last night was a draining experience. Dave had been having serious difficulties in recent weeks, especially in angry, hostile reactions to people. That happened with us, with members of his Wednesday morning prayer group, and most seriously, with those to whom he relates in his work at Hope College. His boss was becoming concerned, as were a number of others. About a week ago, Dave went back to cigarettes and has been smoking quite heavily.

Apparently he was badly abusive to a salesman at work yesterday. When he came home he was contrary, alienated, hostile. Helen and I began to feel sick inside. At first he was defending his actions, still belligerent, but as we explored what was happening he acknowledged that he was getting out of control and had been acting inappropriately. He didn't feel that he could handle work, wanted me to call his boss. He'll be taking the rest of the week off.

I felt numb with sadness and disappointment. The long months of encouraging progress for Dave have built up our hopes that he can make it. Now the prospects look dismal again. It's frightening and discouraging. Something in Dave seems almost driven to destroy the gains he's made—especially his job. It seems like a dreary replay of what happened at employments before. Dave's approaching his thirtieth birthday, along with exciting new job possibilities for Jim and Jon, have seemed to make intolerable for him the thought that he should remain a clerk for years to come. He desperately wants to do something significant, help people, minister in the name of Christ, but fears that none of that will be possible for him.

I went to bed paralyzed with grief, but unable to get it out. I had no heart at all for the upcoming trip, felt I was leaving home with so many agonizing loose ends for Helen and Dave. I felt exhausted, helpless. I had been asleep for perhaps half an hour when son Jim called. Bless him! He had heard of Helen's earlier call to Kathy, was deeply concerned about Dave, and us. His insight, caring, willingness to come down and help, were immeasurably relieving for me.

February 7, 1984 – Woke very early this morning, and wasn't able to get back to sleep. Many things on my mind. Dave has been in Holland Hospital for a week now. He is on heavy medication, depressed about his recent behaviors. He is eating and smoking excessively, but seems lucid and reasonably friendly. We were well impressed with his therapist and have had a good talk also with his counselor. We hardly know what to expect in these next few weeks—it seems that Dave has so many things to work through. Movement toward some new, more independent living situation seems to be one of the key concerns. We feel the pain of what is happening with him, but his being in the hospital, cared for by others, gives us a respite from the intensity of concern we have when he's here.

February 28, 1984 – The future for Dave seems so problematic. It's as though he faces a mountain to climb, or a whole range of them. He's not relating well to people, gets angry with them easily, puts off their efforts to love and care. He's smoking heavily, and eating with such indiscipline that his stomach is distended. He fears going back to work, assuming any responsibility for his life. He doesn't know whether he can function well living at home, but has no other real option. He's extremely vulnerable, it seems, to temptations of all kinds. Our relationship with him had seemed warm and close, but that apparently can change with alarming speed.

Dr. Esau is convinced that Dave can't make it without the nurturing of home ties, and I think he's right. But can he make it here, with all the things he's facing, and with what seems like so little inner strength? Will anything hold? Those questions torment me when I dwell on them.

I think of all the traveling I'll soon be involved in, and of Helen's near exhaustion with the strain of things. It seems impossible. And I'm tired, Lord, tired of this emotional roller coaster we're on, tired of trying to help hold Dave's life together, of sharing his pain and anxiety.

I want to deal with Dave's situation as an opportunity, a place in which God's grace can be sufficient, his glory seen. I want to take it a day at a time, and depend on you for strength, Lord. But the pattern of his problems frightens me, threatens to discourage me. I don't know how much I can hope for, and have some fears about getting my hopes up again.

My stomach is churning right now. I feel numb, sad, weak and scattered. Lord, what wait I for? Are you going to come through for us in this situation? Forgive me for asking that, but I have to admit I'm not sure. I can easily imagine things getting a lot worse. Dave's difficulties could bring all of us more pain and trouble, and the longer they go on, the more unlikely full recovery seems. Maybe we aren't going to see real healing until the resurrection.

But another of God's surprises came along. Dave's fortunes took another upturn.

April 8, 1984 – Dave met with [his employer] today, and plans to start working in the mail room for about eight hours a week to start, four on Monday and four on Friday. He seems content with that, and is doing well.

August 23, 1984 – Dave has had a pretty good spring and summer. He's been back at full-time employment in the Hope College mail room. That has gone fairly well, although he has had some difficulty relating to his fellow-worker there. He will be enrolling at the seminary this fall for two courses, still working at Hope about 20 hours a week. He's ambivalent about this step—feeling it's right, yet apprehensive. He's glad to be moving in this direction, yet struggling with storms of self-doubt. Lord, lead him and help him!

December 20, 1984 – This past Monday Dave led chapel at the seminary. Getting ready for that proved highly stressful for him and for us. After a good first quarter, he has had much difficulty of late in keeping at his studies. The strain of this chapel prospect was part of that, plus his cutting down on medication. He got through the chapel experience well and was much encouraged. He has consented to go back up to 16 mg. of the new medication for these next weeks.

June 8, 1985 – Dave will soon be leaving for a summer at a Bible conference in Luzerne, New York, possibly working on the staff. We feel this is a good step toward independent living. He has some anxieties about it, but is generally positive about going. He thinks that in the fall he will either go to seminary full-time or get a full-time job. Presently he is still having difficulty with self-discipline and he's shown no inclination toward any kind of vocational pursuit except something seminary-related. Yet he isn't sure about being a minister. Lord, give him light and confidence. Help him to identify his gifts and use them to your praise. May he find joy and fulfillment!

January 11, 1986 – Dave has done well in relating to the family, in social interactions, and in spiritual growth. In job readiness, assuming responsibility for his life, and self-discipline he still has a long way to go, but is following a doctor's counsel in working with vocational rehab. He gets discouraged at times, but seems to bounce back from that fairly quickly. It's hard to discern what the future holds for him in terms of vocation and possible marriage. Lord, if there are ways in which we can help, show us how. May we yet see Dave realizing his potential and happy in fulfilling your purpose for him!

April 23, 1986 – Dave continues in the work he recently began in a local restaurant. It has helped him greatly in his sense of identity and self-worth. He tried to go off his medicine a bit prematurely and wanted to stop seeing the doctor, but now sees that those steps weren't best. He longs to be financially independent, to be married, to have a job that wins him respect, but knows that he's making progress in his present work. Help him, Father, to keep moving ahead.

The darkest hour before the dawn.

July 10, 1986 – For Dave, this has been a painful time. He wasn't able to keep working at the restaurant. Getting off the medication, discontent with his wages, difficulty with some of the help made it seem advisable for him not to be there for a while. He had some ups and downs, began to spend a good deal of time at the seminary and the college, showed signs of manic behavior. He began to do some wild talking, got behind in sleep. Finally, with the doctor's help, he consented to be admitted to Holland Hospital to have his medication adjusted and get himself calmed down. He went in about the first of June and was released on the 25th. He remained pretty stable, although he had some run-ins with other patients, was too familiar with some of the female ones.

As it seemed best for him to move toward independent living, he decided to get his own apartment. He worked on that himself, got an upstairs place at 176 ½ W. 17th. He got Jim and Tom, two high school friends, to help him move, worked hard at getting things arranged, seemed happy.

The release from the hospital had been abrupt, though, with little continued support. When Dave talked to the restaurant owner, he learned that they would be hiring someone else. That was a real rejection, even though Dave had shown some ambivalence about going back to work.

Helen went with him last Thursday afternoon to see a doctor at the hospital. Dave wanted to get his medication adjusted, stay in his apartment (although he hadn't been sleeping and seemed in bad shape). Helen felt that because of his behaviors he should be back in the hospital. He became angry with her, and verbally abusive. The decision was made for him to go to the psychiatric ward of a nearby hospital since there were no beds available at Holland Community.

We learned on Saturday that Dave had been transferred to a state hospital. Apparently he had become aggressive (he doesn't remember how it all happened). On Friday morning he was taken in a police car to the state hospital, wrestled into a seclusion room where he had a horrible experience for three days and nights—screaming, pounding on the door, out of control and very sick.

He was let out of seclusion on Monday morning, calmed down, and was almost zombie-like when we went down to visit yesterday afternoon. He was in hospital garb, walking with a slow shuffle, hoarse, spent. He cried when he saw us, said he didn't think he would ever see us again.

In the next few days the court (which is located in the hospital) will decide whether or not he should be kept there. If he were, it would be up to 60 days. The social worker asked us before we saw Dave what we thought would be best—staying there through that period or going earlier back to Holland Hospital. We weren't sure what to suggest. After seeing Dave we were impressed by what a tough place that state hospital is, and how sick Dave is. Lord, what is best?

Today I want to talk to the doctor about it. Will Dave deteriorate more and more at this state institution, or will the jolt of being there possibly move him toward recovery? Would he do better in Holland, hospitalized there and working toward a half-way house? It all seems unclear, and deeply painful. When we think of how well Dave seemed to be doing in March, and what has happened since, we feel weighed down with sadness, disappointment, almost disbelief. Lord, how long?

Life is so good, so full of God's kindnesses, yet right in the midst of it the shared family agony with Dave. Dear God, help him in this dark time, and help us to know how we can best support him and walk with him on the long, difficult road toward healing. In you alone do we set our hope.

15

A Major Turning Point

Bill's journal entries during the next few years report heartening progress in Dave's recovery, leading toward a major turning point.

December 6, 1986 – How much has happened since July! Dave came back to Holland Hospital, stabilized well on lithium and another drug, and was soon back home. In early November he moved into a garage apartment near our home. He had begun work before that (15-20 hours a week) as a direct-care worker at two foster care facilities. He still has many self-doubts and some down times, but on the whole seems more stable and positive than at any time we can remember. He has been able to get on disability payments from the government, which greatly eases his financial plight. Best of all, he seems to be drawing strength increasingly from his own study of the Word and times of prayer.

We have many, many mercies at year's end for which to thank the Lord. Major concerns still on our hearts: Dave's overall health and fulfillment, Jim and Jon entering into all of God's purposes for their ministries, my proposed book on prayer. Lead on, O King Eternal!

January 4, 1987 – Helen and I took a walk with Dave. He spoke of what a good day it had been for him, how he had begun it with the

Word, and with committing himself, his work, and those at the foster care facility to the Lord for his blessing. What a great thing, that Dave should have a day he calls good, with a sense of God's presence!

April 6, 1987 – We were afraid that Dave was on the verge of quitting his job at the foster care facility. That touched off a good deal of sadness and anxiety in me. Helen and I talked a good deal about how we should respond, agreed that I might well talk to Dave about the possibility of a treatment center in Chicago. But last night Dave came by after his shift and seemed more positive. He will not quit, or tell the manager he is leaving, at least until after we all come back from our proposed trip to visit relatives in New York.

May 16, 1987 – A great time in the Word this morning. Reading Psalm 112 convinced me that our developing plans to help Dave with a house purchase are right. We and Uncle Vic will provide substantially, Dave will pay some. A nice little home at 1043 Lakewood Blvd. seems right. We've made an offer and we learned today it has been accepted. Dave can move in as of July 1. Lord, may this step for Dave be a happy move toward adult responsibility, growing confidence and self-esteem. We feel good, as does he, about his having a place of his own.

This move proved to be a significant step for Dave—having his own place. It was almost like a new, hopeful era had begun in his life. Then came another encouragement.

May 29, 1987 – A real breakthrough yesterday for Dave. He went in with me to work at Words of Hope, spent a good deal of time operating the recording equipment while I recorded devotionals. He did well, seemed pleased. An open door for his future work. Praise God!

December 31, 1987 – Dave's house purchase has been a source for him of satisfaction and fulfillment. It feels like "home" to him. He now has a friend living with him as a boarder. This has been a good thing in many ways—companionship, financial help, assistance in work around the house.

Dave is now working about two days a week at Words of Hope. He is chiefly working in the recording studio, learning to use the equipment there, but has also been willing to do various assorted tasks that needed doing. He has shown a stability, inner peace and spiritual growth which are most encouraging. Thanks be to God!

March 23, 1988 – Dave keeps plugging away. He had a minor setback when he cut back on his medication recently, but that has now been restored and he is much more stable and at peace. He continues to work with us at Words of Hope and to enjoy his home. My prayers and faith are being renewed for Dave and his future. Again, thank you, Lord!

November 2, 1988 – Dave continues to show stability, even with times of feeling down. He's gaining confidence in his work at Words of Hope, and has been drawn into the life of our church more fully through a developing friendship with our new minister of music.

January 12, 1989 – Dave continues to do well. He had a good visit from Byron [a college friend] lately, has shown concern for our old friend from Chicago, Steve. He has been given opportunities of narration in connection with some musical programs at the church. The choir director has been great at calling forth Dave's gift in this. It has been a richly affirming experience for Dave—almost a major milestone.

June 11, 1989 – Dave had an accident with his car over Memorial Day weekend. Someone pulled out in front of him on Lakewood Blvd. near Division. His ancient Rabbit was totaled; he got $500 for it. Thank the Lord, he wasn't hurt! Now he has bought a 1985 Beretta, greatly helped by some early distribution of Uncle Vic's funds to each of the sons.

March 3, 1989 – Dave, though with sometimes severe struggles, continues to hang in there. He is growing in his life of intercession and having fun working out with two friends at a health club.

Dave wrote a seminary paper during 1990 called "The Wounded Healer." Here are some excerpts from that:

"The Wounded Healer," Paper for Christian Ministry, March 1990

My wounds: I felt I suffered from not being in touch with my feelings. I felt I didn't know how to satisfy my basic drives in life. I felt that although I knew God I wasn't really experiencing my life in the way that I wanted. I had a hard time with feeling like I was crazy or different. My relationship with a girl made me feel really inadequate. I had the craziness of both wanting to go home and also wanting to take a trip too.

There was a lot of anguish in my life. I felt I didn't know how to have close friendships. I didn't know how best to minister to people. I was afraid that I was hurting people but I knew I didn't want to. I always felt like I wanted to go back in my mind to a time before Billy got sick when things were more idyllic, but I never could manage to get there. It was just sort of a dream to recover some of my lost youthful self, but I didn't know how.

There are still times when I wish I could start all over again. When I think about these things I feel so guilty that voices scream inside my head. Now I keep falling down and I don't know when I will stop falling. I hope that I can grow beyond the sufferings that I now experience. I know it will take effort on my part and help from others who would be wounded healers. I hope to grow to the point where I can be a wounded healer also.

As Dave became more active in the life of our congregation, a staff member asked him if he would be willing to lead a small group of young adults who, like himself, had experienced the struggles of mental illness. Although he didn't have a clear idea at the time of what this would involve, Dave accepted.

This decision in Dave's life was hugely significant. It seemed to start him on the road to becoming what he had longed to be: a "wounded healer." He became a shepherd of the new group, which came to be known as "Dynamics in Living." They met every two weeks. Dave arranged for visiting speakers, facilitated the meetings, often provided transportation. He frequently talked by telephone to other members, took them out for coffee, encouraged them, prayed for them.

Several persons in the group experienced a kind of inner healing through this fellowship and developed enriching friendships. All found in it a haven of understanding and support.

In the midst of this ministry Dave seemed to flourish. He became more and more an other-centered person even as he battled an inner world of self-preoccupation. He was able to form a host of friendships.

Here's how Dave described the origin of that work:

April 3, 1990 – Today I volunteered to facilitate a small group for people who have had trouble with their mental health and need a support group. I don't know who will be in it or how many will come, but I hope we have a good group. I have had a lot of experience with being a mental health patient myself so I have a lot to draw on in leading such a group. I must admit I am a little intimidated by the prospect. I am not really sure what the agenda of such a group should be. It probably can only be defined by the people that are in it themselves.

I have wondered long and hard what it takes for someone to recover from mental illness. It seems like once you are tied into the system and identify yourself as being mentally ill, it is very hard to identify yourself as normal again. The need for medication and for therapy somehow seems to reinforce the system based on dependency rather than from one's good feelings about oneself. It is difficult to find much happiness and positive feelings about oneself when one is identified as being mentally ill. Not only is there social stigma to contend with in society and the work place, but there is also the damage to one's own feelings about oneself.

My big breakthrough in terms of mental health was to be able to identify myself as a normal person in spite of the ongoing symptoms of mental confusion and imbalance. I get frustrated like everyone else with chaotic thoughts and feelings and my world seems to have no purpose or design or order. But as I continue to deal with these thoughts and feelings, and life in general, I find that the picture of the whole is bigger than the sum of the parts. I don't need to be down because I am having crazy thoughts and feelings.

I believe the only real cure for mental illness is living. Every person needs to find their own pace in which they can handle life and other people. Unless a person is able to identify their own world and inhabit that world they will be forever alienated from themselves.

In leading a group on recovering from mental illness and disability, I would like to enable people to come to terms with some of these things and begin to create a world for themselves in which they can live. This doesn't come overnight but takes sustained effort. I believe self-esteem comes from being able to live creatively, discovering one's identify in social contexts, making contribution to others in work and play and being able to enjoy the give and take of loving relationships.

What mentally ill patients most lack, it seems to me, is a broad kind of confidence in themselves. They have a tendency to feel worthless, and they can't cope with positive thoughts about themselves very easily. So they retreat to a world inside themselves. What I would like to do in my small group is to inspire trust and confidence in the participants more than any other goal or program.

16

A Widening Ministry

By 1992, things seemed much better for Dave. Bill writes:

March 20, 1992 – These are good days for Dave. He is taking a course at the seminary, and doing some good reading in connection with it. He works a bit each week with Jim [a high school friend] in tracking mutual funds, and is still facilitating the small group for those who have suffered with mental illness. That is a wonderful ministry. He seems to have a pastoral relationship with several in the group.

During the years that followed, until 1998, Dave wrote very little in his journal. He continued his ministry at Dynamics in Living, had other brief employments, and enjoyed his house and dog (Eureka) immensely. Our trust began to grow again that his worst days were behind him. His own confidence was on the rise.

Note this journal entry from Dave:

October 6, 1998 – I do not think I am mentally ill and really in truth this is more the way I view myself. I'm not incompetent mentally. I'm not emotionally maladjusted, a socially impaired, intellectually, foreign or fringe element; I am able to work, sustain myself personally, manage economically, handle relationships, pastor and counsel, write, lead a support group, sponsor a growing edge of culture, language, means to live, education, welfare, and travel. Basically I'm managing well in more areas of responsibility and duty than many "normal" persons do.

As Dave's restoration continued, and his ministry with Dynamics in Living became more and more fruitful, he was invited by David Bast, Bill's successor as president and broadcast minister for Words of Hope, to do a radio interview. Dave tells in his journal about this opportunity.

August 26, 2002 – Words of Hope—I'm going to Grand Rapids tomorrow. I'm recording with David Bast at Words of Hope. We're going to discuss my group and the work I'm doing to support the mentally ill community. Help me, Lord, to have good things to say. Help me to express the challenge of the future as I see it. Help me to give good credit to those on disability. Help me to express the beauty and the loneliness of mental distress, and help me to be able to encourage those who often find themselves in esoteric frames of mind.

• • •

Excerpts from the Words of Hope Radio Program Interview Aired on December 8, 2002

(Note: Extracts which Dave Brownson read from his journal during this interview are set in italics.)

DAVID BAST: We're thinking about hope today and struggling to find the practical side. As you know, life now can be a real struggle and it has been for you. What does hope mean to you?

DAVE BROWNSON: I think after what I've been through in life, I'm pretty much content just to take life a day at a time, and each responsibility one at a time. I'm not looking for some grandiose scenario in the future that will somehow make me complete or make me more of what I want to be. I know that it's in the day-to-day I find grace. I find the ability to give to others and to find fulfillment for myself.

BAST: So hope is lived one day at a time.

BROWNSON: Yes I think it is. I think that's a more accurate way of looking at it and that is what Jesus taught us about things too. He said that "sufficient unto the day are the troubles thereof."

I love to write. It's helped me to feel better about myself, to believe I have something to say. For a while I had to deal with the subjective sensation that I am "cracked" and that my life is perfectly meaningless because of it. That's why I'm grateful for writing because somehow it processes the feelings—expresses, thinks, and creates hope over again in a new way.

Lord, let me do something for you in light of all you have done for me. Let me be a person who loves you and seeks to please you in all I do. Let me always seek your face. Let me love you with the love you have put in my heart for you. Let me love myself in all my weakness. Let me be borne up on eagles' wings to you to enjoy fellowship with you. Let me remain ever humble and depend on you. Let your name and grace be known through me, a true and radiant testimony.

BAST: It was while you were in school that you first became aware of your mental illness?

BROWNSON: I would say that's true, while I was in college. I think at that time it wasn't so exactly. I didn't have psychotic stimuli, you know, but I had pressure on me mentally and spiritually that made it hard for me to function sometimes.

BAST: What happened then after your college years? What were some of the experiences that you faced?

BROWNSON: I think one of the things that got started in Ann Arbor (and that continued somewhat when I got back here to Holland) was just feeling rejected, feeling like other people didn't really value me or value the things that I was interested in or value my approach to things. I always got a lot of acceptance and love from my family but I didn't always get it from other places.

BAST: That's really tough, isn't it? I guess we don't think about that or maybe realize that, but a person who suffers from mental illness not only has a disease to struggle with but they're a kind of social leper, aren't they? I mean people are uncomfortable with that, and a lot of people will reject them.

BROWNSON: Quite often. Yes, that's true. A person with mental illness can make someone else feel very uncomfortable, yes.

My prayer is that my mental illness will have some use if I am to suffer with it. And I pray that I will be delivered of it. Forgive me, Lord, for its excesses. I am not a son of sorrow but one of the living God, a son of Christian parents, a son of a happy and blessed union, a creature whom God has brought into the world for his own praise and glory. The Lord protects me and watches over me, jealous for my care. The Lord is truly great, truly good. He has an eye for my care.

The Lord is the real secret of my life. He keeps me sane in a confusing world. He gives me peace. He is the light of life. He is kind to me. I take my refuge in him and I know he cares for me, even me. Life doesn't get any easier as I get older. It does get better though. The Lord ministers to us in our sleep. He uses it to build us up, to encourage our hearts, to make us wise.

BAST: You've led this ministry—small-group fellowship, Bible study, prayer support—for persons suffering from mental illness for a number of years now.

BROWNSON: Yes, twelve years.

BAST: Twelve years. It's really neat because the experts tell us that the best way to learn something is to teach it to others. Maybe the best therapy for you has been trying to help and encourage others who have some of the same struggles.

BROWNSON: It is true that when you reach out to help others there's a blessing and a benefit that comes back to you. In a lot of ways I've benefitted as I never would have counted on or thought of. I think it's true too that I can see ways in which others have benefitted from what I've done. And one of the things I've found in my leading this small group, Dynamics in Living, is that there is a kind of solidarity among people with mental illness. That solidarity provides for a lot of nurture, support, and personal growth. That's why I think that the founding of this group and someone asking me to lead it was something the Lord ordained. It was something not just to provide for other peoples' needs but to provide for my needs too in terms of social nurture and that kind of thing.

BAST: Your ultimate hope, your trust and your life are all bound up in your relationship with the Lord, I know that, Dave. What does it mean for you to walk with him even in the struggles that you've had day by day?

BROWNSON: Well, part of what it seems to mean for me is finding him to be faithful. That is always so encouraging and such a blessing to know that the Lord who sees and knows all still cares about me. He helps me to be willing to not just know it, but actually show it. It's hard for me to talk about the Lord sometimes because it means so much to have him in my life. I know that rock-bottom promise that my dad quotes to me is that "I will never leave you or forsake you." You know, here comes this promise sailing out of somewhere reaching us, that God is faithful and that he will never abandon us. And our response is, what have we done to deserve this? How is it that we have come to benefit in this way from this God? And at the risk of being theatrical, I'm just really grateful for God and his work in my life!

The Lord has ministered healing to me of late. I'm more at peace with myself and his place in my life than I've been in some time. My nephews and nieces have had a lot to do with helping me get oriented and assimilated to the world I live in. And my brothers and their wives have really given me very good strong support for my life. I tend to lean on my parents a good bit too. They have been wonderful for me. Thank you for the life you have given me, Lord, its goodness, beauty, and blessing.

• • •

Here are a few of the responses which came in to this radio interview:

A radio listener: This is for me. Thank you so much. I suffer with mental illness. I cried through the whole program but it gives me the hope that I can go on. Thank you so much.

Another listener, a mother: My son is mentally ill and I was very encouraged by the program. I really found hope and was impressed by what you said.

Dr. Truman Esau: Having just read your interview, I am refreshed by memories of the past. Those are deeply imbedded impressions of your integrity, born of your faith and experience. It is with pleasure and pride I consider you my friend.

Dave's ministry also led to opportunities for teaching college classes at Hope College and Grand Valley State University. Here are notes that sketch what he said on those occasions.

My brother Billy: I was exposed to his bizarre behaviors, moods. But this ill child has not embarrassed me. I took him to the second-grade classroom each day. I was in kindergarten. Billy was a character, of course. He always has been a character.

I loved my brother very much. Hence the identification with disabled populations. Very strange what a bad fever can do. Billy's greatness could not be overshadowed by his illness. No person is completely determined by their disability. He was actually one of the funniest and most interesting persons you'd want to meet. Yet half of the brain on his left side was gone due to his fever. It seemed once motor skills were gone he could be forever handicapped, barring a miracle. So we prayed often for a miracle for Billy.

Billy died at 24½. I was 23. The effect of his death on me was dramatic. Billy had been at the center of our family's life. The pressure for me came in knowing I needed to find a life for myself. No time, no energy, no potential for success. Yet I was radically unsure of myself in many ways. I was finishing college without knowing at all what to do next.

Mental illness—I experienced a cognitive gap in trying to reach through it to experience human contact. People who can't control their impulses are anti-social. I was a farce and I showed it, but I've discovered the Lord doesn't leave us. Sometimes we dwell in darkness for years before we can come to the light, the holy light of the Lord. Experience in Christian community brought support and healing.

Twelve years of Dynamics in Living—an attempt to live together, share our lives, bear one another's burdens. Empowerment. Entitlement through meetings. Thank you, Lord. Your plans are good plans, your purposes are good purposes.

Much growth and progress over the years in terms of personal growth, spiritual growth, consolidation of identities both individual and cooperate.

A second life for me—combining ministry with friendship. A door to fulfill a calling, in doing good works among the poorest of the poor. Hope for the hopeless. A balm for the discouraged that inevitably accompanies mental illness at times.

Life is in the living for mentally ill people too. The Lord is working for good in the midst of great difficulty. He loves us. Most of us are not violent, but are honest people who are not normally deranged, especially with the help of medication. I've had my share of delusions, too. My illness has to do with the feeling I'm communicating with others mentally. I've had delusions of grandeur too, sometimes even imagining myself to be God. I've learned the hard way by experience that these concepts are appealing in some ways, but do not really describe reality—me nor my experience and person. I am not really embodied in those delusions as I once was. Life for me at this point has to do with the experience of being a person in the real world. And it has to do with being a person for others. If you can't love your brother whom you have seen, how can you love God whom you have not seen?

The place of research in treating schizophrenia has led to significant help. We are biological creatures, each with a peculiar chemistry and make-up. Each person's brain works a little differently. The new medication has been an extremely valuable drug for me.

Mental illness—conditioned with certain predispositions—emotional and cognitive. Partially the results of choices and experience. No one to be blamed for it. I believe God is using mentally ill people and has a great plan for their lives. Harbinger of a grace to come. Love can heal mental ailments. Love can heal the heart, the mind, the body. Jesus Christ is love, the love offering for the human race. We have found in our group that through love mentally ill people can gain the power to help each other. Love plus knowledge.

17

Last Days

Dave's first warning signs about his health came in the spring of 2002. He was retaining fluid in his body and felt shortness of breath. After being admitted to Holland Hospital he was diagnosed with cardiomyopathy, a weakness of the heart muscle. One of the side benefits of that hospitalization was that he could not smoke cigarettes during it. After he was released, he never smoked again, breaking a habit of some twenty years. He reflects on that in his journal.

July 23, 2002 – Being in the hospital was the big step I needed to be set free from smoking. It seems the difference in the environment led to a freedom from thinking about smoking and then needing to smoke. I seemed to stop thinking about smoking in some miraculous way. Up 'til then I hadn't ever thought of stopping the smoking. At least in a way that gave something else priority, over the opportunity to smoke. And I felt so much better for having stopped, too. I felt like I could breathe better almost for the first time. More than that, like my life had been given back to me, by the Lord!

I really hope I can stay smoke free for a long time. I really don't want to smoke now, but I feel I might at some distant point in the future. This concerns me, and is scary. But life is in the moment, and the moment is now.

The real thing is, I'm not naturally a smoker. And I don't think I wear the habit very well. When I was young I didn't smoke, and those were my more active times. I think it's a substitute for other kinds of pleasures and enjoyments. And I really don't feel I need it anymore.

Dave improved steadily afterwards, and he felt considerably better. He exercised on a number of occasions with his dad in the gym at Freedom Village [the retirement community where his parents live]. Some of his medications, however, contributed to weight gain, which was distressing to Dave, often noted in his journals. That, together with high blood sugar readings from diabetes, began to make exercising increasingly difficult. He was sometimes puzzled about his physical condition.

July 28, 2002 – More water retention in my feet today. It's a little uncomfortable, and is not healthy. Most of the water seems to collect around the ankles.

November 24, 2003 – It's harder for me to bend over and pet the dog than it used to be. I seem to have some circulation problems with the exercise. This is disconcerting because Eureka needs my daily attention. But I think the Lord will make a way! I mainly hope she can get the attention she needs. But it does land me out of breath sometimes.

From Bill

Dave went to see his doctor early on November 25, 2003. He had been struggling with shortness of breath and fatigue. His usual exercise times with me hadn't been possible for a few days. One time before, he had managed to walk only a few laps around the little indoor track at Freedom Village. Later it had seemed too wearying for him even to start. We had urged him to see his doctor.

After checking him, the doctor set up a series of medical tests for Dave to undergo in the coming days. His history of diabetes and cardiomyopathy made this seem wise. That afternoon Dave called back to the doctor's office to express thanks, as he often did, for the care he had been given.

At suppertime, we had two guests from out of town—distant relatives we had never met before. It was Dave's night to eat with us also, so we dined as a party of five. Dave was especially engaging with our guests, showing sincere interest in their lives. He was in good spirits, looking forward to the Hope College basketball game later that evening. For decades, watching Hope basketball teams had been one of his greatest joys in life. He had gone with me to scores of games, as had his brother Billy before him.

After the goodbyes, Dave and I drove to the game in different cars. The Hope team played a brilliant first half against Finlandia College and were ahead at intermission by over twenty points. Dave was elated and said as the half ended, "I think I'm going to head home, Dad." He would often do that when Hope's game was clearly won—or lost. "OK, Dave. We'll see you," I replied.

When I returned home after the second half, our son Jim called on the telephone. "Dad, have you seen Dave lately?"

"Yes, I was with him at the ball game. Why?"

"I just heard from my neighbor. Someone had called him to say that Dave was brought into Holland Hospital, dead on arrival. Could that be true?"

"It hardly seems possible. He was just with me a little over an hour ago. But I'll check."

Stunned, I called the hospital, and asked if Dave Brownson had been brought there. The attendant excused herself, and there was a considerable delay. Finally she returned. "Yes, he was brought in a short time ago. To whom am I speaking?"

"I'm his father. Is it true that he was dead on arrival?" Again a pause.

"Yes," came the answer. "Some ladies from the police department are already on the way to your home."

We sat silent, numb with shock. Then the tears came, the first of many as the evening wore on. Soon the policewomen arrived.

They sensed our grief, and were quietly helpful, expressing sympathy, arranging for Helen and me to be driven to the hospital.

The story unfolded. Dave had left the Civic Center on that cold November evening, and had begun walking toward his car, parked about 75 yards away. Apparently he had suffered a major heart attack and collapsed on the sidewalk. Someone noticed him lying there and ran back to the Civic Center to call 911. Officers in a police car happened to be nearby and rushed to the scene. When they reached the place in what must have been a few minutes, Dave's body had no pulse, no heartbeat. He died almost instantly.

Soon our family—Jim and Kathy, Jon and Jenny—arrived at the hospital with some of their children. It was so good to have them there! But heart wrenching as well. Hugs and tears everywhere, with loud wailing. We had been given a room all to ourselves, and we poured out our grief freely.

How Dave had been loved by his family! The loss seemed overwhelming. Our senior pastor, Mike, came quickly to be with us, and stayed far into the night. His presence and prayers helped to uphold us.

Some time later, the family members were allowed to enter the room where Dave had been examined. His body still had warmth. His cheeks had color. We gathered around him, touched him, kissed him.

Our youngest grandson, Sam, asked if he could remain in the room for a little while after everyone else had left. We assured him that he could, and he lingered there for some time. When he finally came out, he told us why he had wanted that opportunity: "Dave was my best fan when I was playing basketball. He would come to the games, cheer me on, and call me up afterwards to give encouragement or make suggestions. And I never got to thank him. I just had to stay and tell him how much I appreciated all that."

18

In Memoriam

A memorial service for Dave was held at our church. Senior pastor Mike Pitsenberger led the service and preached the Word. Dr. Tim Brown of Western Seminary quoted a number of Scripture passages. Members of the family shared in leading worship by music. Dave's two brothers spoke in his memory, as did his dad. Here are their words:

His brother Jonathan

It was no accident that Dave's heart beat last during half time of a Hope College basketball game. He had played basketball in the same Dutch dome that our son Sam played in just yesterday for a basketball scrimmage. But it would be more fitting to say that he supported and encouraged, upheld and befriended others who played basketball. His heart beat last after doing the thing his heart beat for—cheering other people on.

Dave was a fan. Most of us don't like that role. We want to be out on the court, getting our own playing time, and having our own share of the spotlight, our five seconds of fame. But Dave, by God's grace, was different. Even though sidelined by his mental illness, benched at times by brain-twisting affliction, he was able to shout encouragement to the rest of the team.

Dave did not marry yet he cheered on his brothers who did. He did not have children but he treated his nieces and nephews like his own. Our families were part of his team and he would keep the statistics of our success. "Has Jeannette sold any houses yet?" "When does Sam have his first game?" "So Ben, you wrote a play. What's it about?" "How does Joanna like Hope?" No matter what we did, in Dave's eyes we were always the best. Anna's art, Rachel's poetry, Will's Tae Kwon Do—from Dave's perspective, nobody did it better.

And dear people, all of you who were part of Dave's extended family, you were on the team also. You were on Dave's team. He would discover, wouldn't he, what kind of game you were playing and then he would cheer you on and cheer you up.

If you were one of Dave's Dynamics in Living friends and struggling with mental illness, he would be there for a 2:00 a.m. distress call.

If you were one of his high school friends busy in business, he would talk with you about it over breakfast at one of his many breakfast venues: Dennys, Jackies, Russ's, Schooners. Even if you were hitting the ball off the golf tee and competing against him, he would have an encouraging word.

What was it that made it possible for Dave to be so humble, so kind, so encouraging to others? Better yet, who was it that made it possible? We're going to hear more about that in a moment, but let me suggest an answer out of my own experience with Dave. Jim and Kathy found this bulletin next to Dave's journal. It was the bulletin of my last Sunday at a nearby church, and Dave wrote on it, "Jon's final service. We were there at 8:30, the best church service I've ever been at yet." His gift for understatement! Dave didn't see that much about me or how I delivered a sermon. It was more that he saw *someone*. He saw the person and work of Jesus Christ. And that's what he bore witness to. He was a worshiper of and a witness to Jesus Christ in me.

His relationship to me and to all of us grew out of the soil of his relationship to God. The way Dave loved God determined the way he loved all of us.

Let me close with words from Dave's February 1 journal entry:

It's fine to live life fully for God. You, Lord, give immortality where only death reigned. You alone are the source of life and goodness. All the praise, the honor, and the glory belong to you, Jesus Christ.

His brother Jim

As many of you know, Dave had a powerful philosophical and introspective side to his personality. He had this restless need to understand himself and the world around him. There are 27 volumes of journals stacked up on his shelves just over the last half dozen years or so that bear witness to his articulate quest for wholeness and for meaning in his life. You all will receive some excerpts from them at the end of this service.

And he sometimes directed that analytic energy to his mental illness. He wanted to understand his own consciousness as deeply as he could. And he and I had long conversations about that. He wanted to understand the illness itself. And one of the most surprising things that he said to me about his illness, and I know he said something similar at times to some groups that he would talk to about mental illness, was this: He believed that it was important to recognize mental illness as, the way he put it, "a valid form of consciousness."

Now I have to confess that the first time I heard Dave say that it worried me a little bit. Many mentally ill persons are confronted with a choice about the world that they live in, the world of their own minds or the world of real human relationships. And all too often their minds are a world of confusion and anxiety and terror, though it may also have times of incredible beauty and richness. And I worried at first when Dave said this that it was the siren's song calling him into his own head to a place that would finally leave him again alone and terrified. I had seen him there before and I didn't want to see him there again.

But the more we talked, the more I began to realize that Dave was saying something else. He knew far better than I did the terror and anxiety that his illness brought him. And he knew far more deeply than I how important it was for him to stay connected to the real world, to be engaged in real relationships. And he worked hard to maintain those relationships.

But he was after something different. He was saying that he needed to find a different starting point for thinking about his illness. He knew that as long as his mental state, his consciousness, was defined only as something wrong, an aberrancy, a deficiency, an illness, that his *life* could be little more than an aberrancy, a deficiency, an illness. He needed to find ways to *value* his experience, as strange and quirky and sometimes quite painful as it was. He needed to *embrace* his life, he said, not just live waiting for some better form of consciousness, some more trouble-free existence, to arrive at some point in the future. And that's exactly what he did.

I know that Dave longed, he deeply longed, for experiences in his life that were beyond his grasp. He longed to have children. He longed to engage in athletics as he had in his younger days and was unable to do as he struggled with the aging of his body and the effects of diabetes, an illness, ironically, caused at least in part by the very medications that helped to keep him sane. But I never, never heard him say, "I wish that I had never become mentally ill." I never heard him say, "I wish I didn't have diabetes." For him, that was simply his lot in life.

And he realized, I think, particularly in the last ten years or so, that the way to wholeness was not in denying or regretting or resenting the circumstances of your life that you can't change. Rather, he knew that the path to wholeness lay in treasuring the gifts that he had been given in gratitude and thankfulness, and I can honestly say I know no other human being more grateful for his life than Dave Brownson. Patient endurance and gratitude were the marks of his life. And my prayer is that all of us may be given the grace to bear our losses with such dignity and endurance and gratitude.

His Dad

I'm thinking now of two great joys about Dave's life and two great sorrows. The first sorrow was in a junior high experience that Dave had when two bullies after school beat him up. He couldn't imagine why. He asked them. They said, "It's because your brother is a mental and we hate him." Dave was crushed, came home screaming, beat his head on the pillow. Full of anguish, he said, "I can't believe in a God who would let that happen to my brother."

He went through a difficult period of groping, distancing himself from the family and the faith until two weeks before he was to go to the University of Michigan. It was then that he went to a Bible conference with us and a friend gave him a tape about Christianity and the Eastern religions. He realized that the things he'd been dabbling in had been taking him away from his family and his loved ones. He wanted to "come back home." And here was the first great joy. He became a believer in Christ, and his life was changed. He went to the University of Michigan as a follower of Jesus.

The second great sorrow came five years later, when his brother Billy died. Dave went into a psychotic collapse soon after that. Therapy revealed that he somehow had felt all those years responsible for Billy's affliction. In a childhood scuffle, when he was five and a half and Billy was almost seven, Dave feared that his pushing him off the bed and Billy bumping his head was what had caused the awful losses of encephalitis. He had buried that inside, and it all erupted when Dave learned about his brother's death. He went through a long period, maybe a dozen years, one hospitalization after another, sieges of incredible suffering and inner torment. And we got to the place where we would have been happy if Dave could have one day free from that misery.

Then began about 1990 the second great joy, a long, slow road to recovery. He became involved in a group of others like himself who had gone through mental illness, that's now called "Dynamics in Living." Dave discovered there a wonderful outlet for his ministry. He longed to be able to minister, he longed to be able to serve, and this began to be a way.

As time went on, in a most unpredictable, unimaginable way, all of this suffering, all of this brokenness, all of these losses and disappointments, instead of making him bitter and causing him to withdraw, made him this marvelous person who reached out to others with such love and encouragement, who was so deeply grateful for everything done for him, who cherished relationships and became a Jesus-like person. And I ask myself, as Jon did, how that could happen. Well, it happened in part by friends like you who are here. It happened in part by family members who loved him and supported him. But that doesn't go the whole way.

It happened because out of his brokenness, when he felt so condemned and haunted by fears that he would be destroyed, that the wonderful good news of the gospel dawned on him that he was greatly loved, that Jesus died for him, that nothing would ever separate him from God's love. And as that sank into his heart and blossomed forth in his life, he became the beautiful person that you folks here know him to be. So we say thanks to God. Thank you, Jesus, for making him the person he was, and thank you, each one here, for the way your presence expresses what Dave meant to you. All glory to God, to the Lamb that was slain, for the person Dave became.

Later reflections from his Mom

I have asked myself why Dave succeeded in triumphing over his mental illness. What were the factors that enabled him to make it in the world after months of hospitalizations, scores of attempts at various jobs, and frustrating tries at further education? I believe the following factors made for his enduring joy in life:

- Though he was never fully free of his "voices," his determination to ignore them and reach out to others enabled him to live successfully.
- He owned his own home. His uncle helped him to buy a little house which he loved and where he could retreat for quiet and rest.
- He had a dog, Eureka, who responded to his love and attention and gave him daily joy.
- He stayed in touch with all his family and ate at least two meals a week with us, his parents.
- He finally yielded to receiving disability and gave up trying to hold a job.
- He developed a huge list of friends and contacts. When plagued by his illness, he chose to ignore the voices and reach out to others by phone calls, personal visits, and lunches. He met with the rich and poor, the lonely and oppressed, the well and the sick. He made no distinctions in his relating to persons and accepted everyone unconditionally. He saw this as his ministry and felt called to it.
- He managed his own affairs, his car, his finances, his bills; maintained his home and car, and other demands on his life.
- He wrote profusely—over 27 journals, some of over 200 pages. Writing was his chief therapy and he found great benefit in getting his thoughts on paper—at all times of the day or night.
- He arrived at the best medication for him after experiments with various treatments.
- He loved golf and spectator sports.
- He developed a close relationship with Jesus Christ and became a man of prayer and of the Word of God.

Excerpts from letters to the family after Dave's death

From one of Dave's therapists: I was shocked to hear of Dave's unexpected passing. I will always treasure my time with him—he taught me so much. It is a comfort to know he's in heaven.

From Hope College's basketball coach: We are all sorry about Dave's death. He has always been such a special friend and encouragement to me.

From a classmate: We miss Dave. He was a friend to our family who will never be forgotten and will always be remembered. Dave was always the one to phone us Saturday morning and ask how everyone in the family was doing. We'll miss that. He cared about other people's lives and about us. He was truly special.

From a friend who is a physical education teacher: I just want you to know that Dave played a significant role in my life the last three years. He encouraged me and cheered me on, before and after my amputation. He was truly a man of God and a great friend.

From a Hope College professor and his wife: We have just returned from a thanksgiving visit in Minneapolis. We heard of Dave's death as we were starting our return. It was such a shock to us, and our son is just devastated. We are trying to help him through this but we too know what it's like to lose your best friend. Dave was that to our son plus he was one of the very kindest and most loyal men we've ever met. We feel that we were all very fortunate to have known and loved Dave. His example of acceptance and caring for our son has given him wonderful chances to be a better person. As parents we hope you can smile with the memory of what a wonderful son you raised and all the good that he could do while he was in our midst.

From a pastor: First, Dave was a member of my class at WTS. He always offered such insightful questions. I admired his intellect and wished some of the Brownson brains might rub off on me.

Second, I played ball with Dave nearly every Friday during my seminary days and he was a fierce competitor. I preferred to play with him rather than against him. Third, I was lovingly corrected by Dave . . . He met with me and helped me understand God's role in my brother's accident. I'm grateful that he sent Dave to help me in my time of grief.

From the vice president of a local company: Dave was a dear young man. He always made me feel special, always was genuinely interested in me and our family and always asked insightful questions. I will miss him. He would often leave encouraging messages on our voice mail which always made me smile. He was a sensitive, caring, loving friend.

From a psychology professor: I was stunned to learn that Dave passed away and also that I had missed his funeral. I so wish I could have been there to tell Dave's family and friends how much Dave meant to me and how much he has contributed to my students over the years.

From a retired minister: On the Monday before his death, Dave made one of his regular calls to me. He inquired about my health and celebrated my blessings with me. When I asked about his circumstances, he told me he wasn't experiencing the best of health, but then he moved on with an optimistic tone. How I have valued those calls, and this one in particular!

What a good man he was! What an instrument of Christ's love! He suffered regret at the limitations of his life. But few in my experience have been better witnesses to the providence of God and the power of faith. Whenever Dave comes to mind now, I rejoice at full potential realized, every disappointment wiped away, every accusing voice silenced, all darkness changed to light.

Thanks be to God who gives us the victory through our Lord Jesus Christ!

From Truman, the first psychiatrist who ministered to Dave: Our hearts have been with you in your pain. During these last several days,

I have been reflecting on the years of Dave's ministry. What I marvel at is the mystery and the wisdom of the Lord's providential care. Pain accompanies such a journey, guided by his providence, but the depth of insight and closeness to God that he forms in us is worth it.

How clearly I recall Dave's integrity at Old Orchard Hospital and since to dig out the issues that had plagued him those many years. It shocked us all as he recalled bouncing on the bed with his older brother the night before the measles came and how he concluded, as children do, that he was responsible for Billy's subsequent disabilities. The hard work you all did as a family held Dave, even during his frustrating efforts to make it in seminary. But Dave, despite those difficulties, was helped to form a ministry of such a unique quality and nature that Jesus was certainly honored. Dave reached out to the forgotten, the lost, giving them the comfort wherewith he had been comforted. He ministered where the church knows not how to go.

I am so grateful for having been a part of that process and now sharing the pain and the certainty of Dave's state now.

(Later letters from Truman): I was so touched by Dave's deep searching, both for his own life but always for others. He turned his own pain into gifts to others, always aware of the gracious mercy of his heavenly Father. I shall never forget his remarkable gifts of caring and reaching out with genuineness to others, whom he understood better than most. His understanding of the Lord's grace shone through. I know he struggled with letting go of goals that he aspired to, but in the process he found a ministry that is so rare and so authentic. How marvelous is God's providence! We deeply love you both.

Dave Brownson stands out as a most remarkable man, Christian and patient. It was my privilege to be there as Dave unraveled the origins in early childhood of his identity confusion, compounded by his brother Billy's encephalitis. A little boy who was so attached to Billy had little alternative but to self-blame, as he was still doing when hospitalized. He grew in knowing who he was and to whom he belonged. In my opinion that was the major factor in his remarkable life. Losing Billy, he found his family. His spiritual growth penetrated and motivated those bonds.

From Steve, Dave's long-time friend and classmate: I just wanted to let you know what Dave meant to me. Dave and I became best friends back in grade school. He loved to play basketball and we were both very competitive. Our friendship lasted all through middle school and high school. Starting guards almost entirely from seventh grade on. Our friendship continued . . . We have had a lot of good talks about many things. In fact, not too long ago, I had mentioned to Dave that I thought he was really the "rich guy" of all our friends because of his relationship with Jesus.

I think through all those years the thing I treasure most is the fact that Dave was my best friend all though school and I considered him my best friend before he died. There aren't many people out there who have had a good friend for that many years. Dave surely kept a lot of people together. Never, never did he have a bad thing to say about anyone! He was such a kind person. I believe out of all this that Dave was a witness for Christ in all of our lives. He left . . . myself and others a better understanding of Christ. I believe that part of Dave's job on this earth was to bring many of his friends closer to Christ.

Dave's dear friend and chief colleague in ministry: Dave Brownson, my friend and head of our mental health group, Dynamics in Living, was incredible. He had a terrific sense of humor and was a friend to all of us with real warmth and understanding. He lined up excellent speakers and led lively conversations. Dave would add suggestions with beautiful God-formed ideas to help us. He led our group since 1990 and will be remembered for his kind wisdom.

From a member of the counseling staff at our church: Dave truly was a consummate friend. He was a wonderful encourager. He would be specific in his encouragement which adds so much legitimacy to the comments. And he was very kind.

Dave held a unique position in the community with friends from all walks of life, and in that way helped to unite people. He served as such a strong advocate for those who struggle with mental and emotional challenges. He helped others recognize the humanity and intelligence of those so afflicted . . . He will be sorely missed.

Later thoughts from Dave's brother, Jonathan: Less than a month before Dave died, he attended the last service I preached in Hamilton, Michigan, on October 23, 2003. In the few short weeks that followed he would often refer to that service in superlatives. He was an extraordinary support to me in the pastorate. I could do little wrong in Dave's eyes. So, it was only fitting that he should share and be there for my final service as an ordained pastor of that church.

I was to discover, however, that Dave's support would extend beyond my work as a pastor to my work as a pray-er. Dave knew when I left that church my heart was to be devoted to "prayer and a ministry of the word." Dave schooled me in that passion by praying for me personally over the phone after we would talk. He knew I had a heart for prayer. I believe he knew it right up until the last beat of his own heart.

What I didn't know, however, was that Dave would help make it possible for me to follow my heart. Dave had talked with Mom and Dad and decided to name his two brothers as the sole heirs in his will. This included his house. Dave's inheritance put food on our table. It also made it possible for me to begin a self-funded position as Minister for Prayer in the Reformed Church in America. Without Dave's death, the Minister for Prayer position—the first ever in 377 years of history in the Reformed Church in America—would not have been brought to life.

Epilogue

One of the ways in which Dave's influence lives on is in a program called "Friends." Those who had loved and appreciated Dave gave to his church a very generous sum in his memory—the largest ever received there in memorial gifts. With these funds, a program coordinated by the church, along with Community Mental Health and Cornerstone Drop-in Center, now serves young adults who have experienced mental illness. Caring Christians are coming alongside these persons, building relationships, giving encouragement, sharing life, becoming friends. One young man, through this ministry, has already experienced a wonderful restoration, and will soon enroll in college. It's the kind of one-on-one caring that Dave offered to so many so remarkably.

In the summer after Dave's death, his golf buddies Jim, Steve, and Tom, along with others of his friends, arranged a golf tournament "in loving memory of our dear friend, Dave Brownson." Friends came long distances from all over the country to join in the event, one driving for several hours.

Dave was laid to rest in Alamo, Georgia, in a cemetery near the old home place. Buried there before him is his great great great great grandfather, Farquhar McRae, his great great great grandfather John McRae, his great grandfather and great grandmother John and Pearl Clements, his grandfather and grandmother William C. and Juanita Brownson, two of his cousins, and his brother Billy.

The old home place had been built by John McRae in 1870, and Dave was one of the sixth generation to stay there. When it was sold in 2000, the new owner made the house on Cotton Acres into a funeral home. A memorial service for Dave was held there, in the very room where his dad had slept during boyhood years.

Dave's last resting place is right beside his beloved brother Billy. On Billy's gravestone: "For Christ's Glory." On Dave's: "God's Encourager."

Dave's Journal Excerpts

Here are some choice excerpts from Dave's 27 journals—thousands of hand-written pages!

About writing

I love to write. I'd say for quite a while I've liked to express myself in writing. It's helped me organize my mind, I know that. It's helped me to feel better about myself, to believe I have something to say. It's the act of writing more than its content that keeps me going, makes me feel productive. I don't believe it's useless for me or for anyone else for that matter. But I wouldn't try to defend it in a court, or before God's throne.

I seem to outgrow my thoughts and feelings quickly after writing them, but on returning to them later I find things of interest and merit in them. The word is like a living reality that always seeks new forms of expression and content, so I guess it is not surprising that my literature and my relationship to it should be so full of death and rebirth, mirth.

I use words to bleed the venom from my veins. I write like a blind man who can't even see what he is writing, let alone have any comprehension of it. Words seem to separate and dangle from the writer's pen. Sometimes they settle like ink on the page, sometimes evaporate into thin air, sometimes take on a presage for something else, like a slightly different thought or perception, which makes it all change anyway.

- The proper place of literature—to communicate grace and peace.
- To use words to entertain and instruct.
- To be used of the Holy Spirit.

- To communicate without sound.
- To hear the business of the place and to tell it.
- To encourage, and to impart faith to the reader.
- To reconcile, to bring together disparate parties.
- To communicate the knowledge of God, the way of Christ.
- The written word moderates the spoken word.
- Scripture does this supremely, setting forth our foundation for faith and practice.

Writing; pen, ink and paper, is a most wonderful art and exercise, both physical and mental. People have largely forgotten the beauty of the enterprise. I guess I'm largely a relic from a previous age. Everything is done with computers now and will be even more in the future, in all likelihood. This to me seems a terminal nightmare. It seems very little thought is given to the quality of life in the mad dash to produce technology, which will capture the market share.

I find writing to be very helpful and therapeutic. In experiencing myself I seem to gain some control of my mood and emotion, and I'm able to direct it and orient it in a positive direction. I'm glad I have this outlet for my feelings. "My power is made perfect in weakness."

Memories of Billy

December 19, 1999 – 1959, the year (my 6th) when Billy got sick. It was a long time ago. The memories seem hazy now. Billy was a beautiful young boy, a friend to all. I idolized him in many ways. He was the leader of our young family, very bright and very gifted.

What a tragedy that such a bright young man should become ill and lose so much of what he had. He couldn't walk, and he just wasn't the same mentally. He had become so different. He became hostile, anti-social, which he had never been before. It had a shattering effect on our family. We almost felt we had all lost the best thing we ever had. We felt we had been cursed. I remember telling my dad I could not believe in a God who would let this happen to Billy. But I guess what I really meant was "How could he let this happen to me?" I lost my brother, who had been the best thing that ever happened to me, at a very young tender age. It is a scar that has not healed. The pain lingers, remains. It's the main reason why I became mentally ill myself. Perhaps to lose myself and find him somehow. To understand the state of his mind, to identify with him and his strange behavior, to somehow love him more.

Things are different now. Billy has been gone for over 22 years. I believe he is at rest now. I believe he is working for a better world, like I am. Billy was a good sort, even after his illness. He was a lot of fun, and I'm sure he still is where he is now. I miss him. I love him very much. I hope to see him again someday. It will be a happy time. The hope of the resurrection is such a broad hope, so inclusive, so very Christian. We all need this hope to manage day to day. I'm hoping it comes soon. Every day I look forward to it. Suffering has a way of rotting your soul. It needs to be at home, at rest. I think when I see Billy again in the New World, I will be at rest. God bless him. A great and noble soul. Soon we will be together at last. Amen.

I never had these pages flow so smoothly from my pen and mean so much to me. Billy really was, and is, a wonderful character. It will mean so much to have our family reunited again. Love lives on. My hope is not just for our family, however. That everywhere, with everyone, there would be hope and peace this Christmas. That the joy of Jesus would abound and abound. That all would have enough; be satisfied. Grief has been long and hard, a hard teacher. We all need a little satisfaction of soul. Hope has a way of renewing us, bringing us more of what we need and want. It will be a good day. Better days are on the way. We are only a beginning, a new start at life. We are at the beginning of a long, wonderful journey. We will be at rest.

September 5, 2001 – Billy would have been 49 today. He's been gone for over 22 years. I know he's at home. Someday I'll see him again. This is a great encouragement to me. Praise God he's home!

He has lived half of his life in heaven, almost. He lives in our hearts and memories. It is great to know he is with Jesus now. I worried a lot about him while he was still here. I would pray often for his healing. He went to heaven before it came. He slept away in peace. He was a good worker, a great friend, and a beloved brother. He was loyal to us, and to his teams. He had more courage than most people know. He could be very bold and uninhibited. But most of the time in his latter years he was a lot of fun and very easy to get along with.

I know he has gone before me into heaven for a reason. I know he'll always be a little ahead of me, calling me onward.

Billy accepted people at face value. He didn't judge people according to social class. I'm still trying to learn the lessons he taught me.

Dave's dog Eureka

Eureka. Super dog. All that energy and vitality in a small package. A real home to come to. A wonderful companion to have and to hold. A good stimulus for a lot of fun, interesting activity. She's a wonderful dog. Life is a blessing.

It is not an indignity to be a dog, a canine. Dogs are very wise, very meek, very kind. My dog a very weak dog? A little like me perhaps? She has a dominant attention span. She has command. Command of herself and her environment.

Eureka has meant the world to me in many ways. Having someone here with me has been a life saver, and she is so good, loving, free. I really love her, and I'm grateful for her. She is a wonderful dog and pet. She has so much heart. A gift from the Lord and my mother.

I wish I didn't have to leave Eureka alone so much. I think she does OK, just sleeps mostly, but nonetheless I worry and I want the best for her. Maybe I can take her with me more often. I'll have to see. Lord, take care of my little dog when I'm not here.

Dynamics in living

There were just about the right number of people at my party last night. A full house, yet not crowded. I was busy, working pretty fast.

Kind of a nice occasion. Emotionally I tended to fluctuate a good bit, but I think my work made people feel at home and enjoy themselves. People, even at parties, tend to behave a lot like children that need to be taken care of and loved. I guess I'm a little bit like a father or big brother to the group and the people in it. It is a good opportunity for service, and I don't regret it. I found it to be emotionally demanding though. I could handle it but I was getting sparks flying through my brain at times. It is demanding trying to be a kind host to that large a group of people.

No messes to clean up last night. Getting things cleaned up was a breeze. Eureka a big hit with everyone. I love this life. I love these people. I want these good things to last. A bit of work for quite an end. Quite a Pearl Harbor Day.

Thanks so much for Dynamics in Living, and the help you have been to us and those we come in contact with. Bless our meeting tonight with your presence and our hope in you. Give me skill to lead the meeting and to bring good out in others, helping them to connect with you and with each other. Help me to find the love, the joy, the peace you give. To share it with others.

You shall know the joy of Christ. A good meeting tonight of Dynamics in Living. Good sharing, and the speaker gave a good testimony and history. I feel these meetings serve a good purpose for those who come, and for our guests. We are a good resource. We provide a place of peace and a source of comfort to people. It is a place where group members can address their problems. A place of intercession and concern too.

I say I work for the mentally ill, on behalf of society. I say I give my time, energy, and help to people who are marginalized by society, who are not thought of as desirable employees, and who need some strength and dignity to be able to make the best of their lives. Who indeed have a great contribution to make to our society but have been completely overlooked and underestimated. Together we have been fostering a culture of vast proportions. We have identified what community means in a small-group setting, and we are effective in employing this idea. We are only simple people but sometimes simple people learn to conquer with the help of others. We have the help and the support of many people in the general community as well. We could not begin to do what we do without their support.

Discouragement and depression

I don't want to get real discouraged anymore. It is the hardest thing of all to deal with. The Lord really helps me with this. Discouragement and depression have been the biggest problem in my life, and a frequently occurring problem at that. Almost every day for a very long time one thing or another has just made me very dangerously discouraged about myself and my life mainly. Sometimes things other people do bring me down and make me feel pretty hopeless and powerless, but the main problem has been me feeling discouraged about my life, my future. Whether I have the capacity to make myself happy. But as I go on I realize I'm not exclusively dependent on myself for my own happiness. And the happiness that others bring to me is lasting and enduring. All kinds of smaller creatures really help too.

It seems I don't have a problem to worry about anymore. What a change! It seems to me that for a long time I've always been worried about something; the state of the world, the state of my soul, my eternal destiny or just plain everyday kinds of concern. It's nice to be free from worry. I almost feel guilty about it. Anyway, it's kind of a funny feeling I have. Almost as if I've lost something, something that has been so native to me for so long I just took it for granted.

I really am no longer under any compulsion to feel or be anxious anymore. I can just function normally, as others usually do. It is hard for me to quite say how long and how many ways this anxiety and fear has been affecting me. Almost as long as I have been mentally ill, and surely longer. Thirty years of having radical anxiety in the side of my stomach. At least. It seems hard for me to remember when I didn't have some kind of feeling down there, of agitating concern. It is good to feel like I have more control over why and how I will be anxious, and more freedom from that little trickle of a feeling that seems to trigger me into those sets of feelings. Listening to the White Sox games has brought sanity to me.

It's almost as if a dark cloud is always hanging around my head, making even the simplest of tasks very hard to perform. The track record of my life does not really read like a success story. If anything at all it is a testimony to the glory of God in the face of Christ. I really haven't been able to do too much on my own. I seem to find more ways to fail than most people find ways to start.

Marriage

I'm not likely to get married. I don't know why exactly. It's kind of a mystery. I'm not opposed to the idea, but there really never has been anyone who either fit the bill or wanted to marry me. I'm used to being alone. I'm not bored. I have a full life. But I don't really understand this, and I probably won't for some time.

I wanted to marry and have a family too. But I have never really been presented with the opportunity. At this point it appears unlikely that I will ever be able to marry and have children. I'm getting older, 46 now, and finding a bride becomes more difficult at this age.

The single men in Ann Arbor used to say, "Make the Lord your treasure." Well, the Lord certainly is the greatest treasure.

Loving and serving others

It is a *privilege* to serve others, and in so doing to wait on the Lord. Although it may not be directly waiting on the Lord, it is a sign of our faith to care for others. "Inasmuch as you have done it unto one of the least of these my brethren, you have done it unto me" (Matthew 25:40).

The main object of life is not to rate high on a scale of productivity. Rather it is to serve the Lord, and bear fruit.

- It's hard for me to be patient. I seem to get rushed out.
- I need to love more, and be loved.
- I need to love with sincerity.
- I need to love with and in the truth.
- I want to pour out my soul for others.
- I want to give myself on behalf of others.

I have worked hard for the Lord. It is time—I've been feeling today like there is reason for some confidence in life and in myself, and especially in Christ, his atoning work and saving grace. I love the Lord. I need to share God's grace with others. I want to love, *deeply love others.* I don't really want to be known as crazy, stupid, or ineffective personally. I want to enjoy the Lord's world, and play golf till the cows come home. I want to pray and intercede for others as much as possible.

But laying down your life for others works in many ways. Not just in the closeness of family, but in relationships with a wide spectrum of friends and relatives. Laying down your own life and your own concerns is a daily task, a service we render ultimately to Christ, which he commands and which he rewards.

The ability to love is what makes a person human. The reality is love and my experience of it is what gives me hope when I feel bereft of comfort. I think I am encouraged and quite enthused with the reality of love. I know I am able and capable of love. Sometimes I feel it is missing and that makes me blue. I sometimes think I can carry others to this idea of love, that it is my great mission in life. There is nothing greater than the experience of love, of giving, voicing it. There must be something more I'm headed for in the way of love. I'm not sure where I'm going but I know the way.

Learning to live

I am finding a way to live with the Lord, with others, and with myself. It takes a good bit of work, adjustment, assimilation, and trust. It takes a will to persevere, a desire to succeed in life. Most of all it takes the Lord's grace, his presence.

I seem to be able to right myself more easily than I have been able to in the past. I no longer feel a need to put myself down when I have negative feelings. I'm able to let them ride. I'm able to feel better when I want to feel better. This has been a big change for the better in me lately. I am very happy that I'm managing better, and I hope it can last.

Inner voices

It seems like my voices are always trying to play a head game, a game of one-up-man-ship, with me. Maybe I'm really always just playing games with myself. It seems as if my head is just swimming with a lot of different ideas and cross-currents lately. My mind is a playground for anyone with a creative idea. The voices have a way of dramatizing and exaggerating my thoughts into kind of a mental event, an almost purely mindless way of entertainment.

I'm not destined to tragedy, or a terrible life. I'm destined to hope, the hope of the gospel. I grow weary sometimes of living in a verified environment in my mind where I am always subject to negative influences from outside my mind. It's very hard to cope with. They always throw you a hanging curve ball, testing you to see if you'll swing at it. For the life of me I never know who the little voice is anymore. I only know it is very obnoxious and irritating, to say nothing of evil, divisive, and overly critical.

Holland, Michigan

Holland is sure a great place to live. So many good friends and associates. I can't imagine living anywhere else. People tend to settle down and stay here. There is a wonderful sense of permanence and continuity here, as well as a strong civic spirit. Hope basketball is one of the great traditions of the town. It's so good to see people you know at the games, to greet them and be greeted. Hope basketball is great entertainment. Our coach always fields great teams, and the fans are so loyal and vocal. We always have a great time at the games. When you think about what a big event these games are, you have to think about God and how good, gracious, and generous he is to give us this kind of blessing.

Sometimes today I have felt like I have weathered the worst life has to offer and have somehow survived. How, or why, I don't exactly know. But I have lived here in Holland, met the daily challenges of the world, lived with and loved many people, built up the church, written daily, engaged in many conversations, played golf, led a support group, and been a source of help and inspiration to others. But as for me, I simply enjoy life and find reward and happiness in meeting life's challenges, and coming out a winner. Can it be? Is this what is really real? I believe so. I love and have a heart for all the great people in my life, in my town, and in the world!

Parents and family

I stood up at my brother Jon's wedding. I was the best man. We cried when Jeannette came down the aisle in her wedding gown. It was a really wonderful occasion. I don't know how I managed to do all this, given the psychotic condition I was in. I had to get all dressed in rental tux. It cost about $50.

Actually, I model myself after my dad and regular study of the Lord's teaching in the Scriptures. Of course I'm a little different from Dad. I'm my own man in a real sense. I have felt a bit unreal lately though. What's disconcerting is doing something new, experiencing something different than you have before. You find a need to account for it after a while, to assimilate it into your identity and make it a working proposition for yourself. This takes some effort and work.

It is really encouraging to hear your own brother preach the gospel with real heart and fervor. It's hard to describe just what this did for me yesterday. Jon is not afraid to preach the Word. He is a good man, an uncommonly good man. What a blessing to my heart my brother is. He is really a great preacher.

Thank you, Lord, for my family.

My niece and nephews are a special gift to me.

I had a nice visit with Joanna over the phone yesterday. She seems to do so well. She is a really great young lady. I also talked to Will for a while. He is a very nice, helpful young man.

Mom is really good to me. She is such a great lady. She has good wisdom. She is very discerning spiritually. She helps me all the time, and she helps me every day.

I pray for Ben, that he would walk with you while at Northwestern College. Prepare him for service to you there. Thank you for a good summer at Geneva for him. I pray for Anna, that she would have maturity and grace in her new situation. That her time at college would be productive and useful for her. Thank you for your grace in our lives and in our family.

Rachel is quite a beautiful girl. She is so sweet and lovely. She is gifted. I really am blessed to have such a loving, caring family. I'm glad I have the respect and loving treatment of my family. It means a lot to me in my life.

I tend to lean on my parents a good bit too. They have been wonderful for me. But thank you for the life you have given me, Lord, its goodness, beauty, and blessing. I love my nieces and nephews. They are such great young people. So beautiful and colorful. They are really good to me too. I feel like I'm very involved in their lives, especially spiritually. They are such neat children.

I had a nice dinner with Dad and Mom. They are such good, supportive people. They really helped me with some feelings I was having. They helped me to feel my life has been good, worthwhile, and helpful for others. Not only that, but that I had been patient and long suffering with my own illness and that of others.

My dad really loves me. He intervenes for me and my welfare. He provides for me in many ways. He is wise. He is a very accepting person, perhaps the most I have ever seen. He really loves life, loves people, loves his family. He shot 41 on the Legion's toughest nine yesterday. He is still strong at 73. He is in great physical condition. He encourages me, and yet allows me to be me.

Lunch at Freedom Village, then a nice time with family from 2:00 – 3:00. Our family ties are special. I always leave them feeling glad and encouraged. I am indebted to my family for the love and support they have given me over the years. They have been very kind to me. Accepting of fatness, encouraging of my successes. They have stood by me through thick and thin. They are true friends, true disciples of Christ.

I experienced a sense of belonging to them today. A sense stronger than a pat get-together. I felt as if I really was just one of the members of the family, not having to stand out and be unique. Not having to assert myself in order to state my identity, but just participating in the process that was going on. It was fun. I had a good time. Kathy and Jeannette are both very funny and entertaining at these times.

My mom really loves me. She is really in my corner. She is a big help to me. It gives a man a lot of strength to have a good mother. She is a very wonderful woman.

My mother and her ways of kindness. My father and his wisdom and keen insight. The wonder of Hamilton and Jon Brownson's service there. Jon's goodness to me. The splendor of heaven, and my love for Billy. The good working of my car, and the Lord's provision in caring for it.

It's Jim's birthday today. He is 47 today. He is a very good man, full of the Spirit, doing good works and showing kindness to others. He's been a great friend to me, helping me in many ways. He stood by me in my darkest hour, and brought me through.

I meet today with my brothers, Jim and Jon, for breakfast at Jackie's. I'm looking forward to it. They are really great men, good brothers. Jim is the same age as me today, until my birthday tomorrow. Jim is really an incredible guy. Jon isn't so bad either. I sometimes feel kind of diminished around them. They are public people, while I tend to be private and operate on a smaller scale. My proficiency in life is rather limited when compared to my brothers, who are very competent ministers, as well as being family men. I'm just glad to be included and to be as well thought of as I am by them. They really treat me well. Thank you, Lord, for my family, for my brothers. They are such good men. I'm glad they are my brothers and my friends. I couldn't ask for any better brothers even if I wanted to. They are very loving and kind, very devoted to their families and co-workers. Very good men.

I'm still marveling over how good a ball player Sam is. He is so quick, such a good defender. Maybe the other team's guards were sub-par, but Sam really put on a show. He stole the ball five times in the space of two minutes. While he didn't score a lot, he had a number of nice passes for easy buckets for teammates. He is going to be an excellent player someday! He already is very good, fun to watch.

Lunch today with my brother Jim. What a fine man he is. He is a really great brother. I appreciate him more all the time. He is loyal, considerate, friendly, and kind. He is a big help to me in my moods too.

I thank the Lord for my brother Jon, and for his love and support for me. Thank you, Lord, for my family, their great love for each other and for you foremost.

Pain and suffering

I see my *pain and suffering* and its resolution as a vehicle or tool to enable me to understand, help, love others who have also suffered with the suffering of Jesus. The opening of the heart of God.

The suffering I experience is hard sometimes, but it is really nothing compared to what the Lord suffered for me. I suffer a lot of guilt over my crazy activity of mind. Things I think but don't want to think haunt me. I know the Lord understands, and forgives me, but it also makes me feel like I'm out of control and that I cannot be a good Christian while this is going on.

I am loved, I am accepted in the Beloved. The Lord is working in my life a thing of beauty and grace.

Golf

I hit a lot of odd shots today, shots I don't normally hit. I topped a number of chips too, which I don't normally do. I didn't have any rhythm out there. Emotionally I felt a little jaded, or at least raw. I was experiencing more personal trouble than I ever have on a golf course. Hopefully next week will be better. I don't know if I can take another round like this one. It was punishing. It really took the starch right out of me. I felt a little like I couldn't go on another step, for fear of apoplexy.

I guess I really am doing pretty well for 50 or so. I've played a lot of golf, and seen some improvement. I enjoy playing golf, even if I'm not the best. I like the camaraderie, I enjoy being out in the open air, I like the feel of a really good shot, and I like the carts too. Golf is a lot of fun. I like taking a spiritual approach to it too. It is a good theater for prayer and spiritual discipline.

My golf game is in need of repair.

Mental illness

Dizziness for me. Cognitive and spiritual dislocation seems to predicate a terrible kind of dizziness in my head. The thought of earthquakes this time raised dizziness like a five-bell alarm in my head. It takes quite a while for me to regain my composure after such an episode. This dizziness sets me back about 3,000 years or so. It renders me completely non-functional both mentally and physically. I've never seen anything like it. It seems to start in the mind more than the body. It hinders any activity. I can still think and write, but I can't take any initiative. It acts as a curb on thoughts and feelings about my future or my destiny here on earth. All I can really do is lie down afterwards. And I did, from 7:00 a.m. to 8:15 a.m.

It seems as if regularly I'm more beaten on the inside then I am on the outside. The letdown has more to do with my own feelings about myself than it has to do with the way I'm being treated. People don't ignore me, they love me, treat me well. It's all my well of psychosis.

I have been involved with and worked so intensely with the mentally ill population over the last 10-12 years. It somehow makes me feel like being a bit crazy is the norm rather than the exception in life. But they are people too, who are very normal in a lot of way. Flying pretty high this summer as far as my normal moods are concerned, which is nice. I have been less depressed, I think, than earlier years in my house. Part of it has to do with getting older, more mature, more able to fend for myself. Has to do with less violent mood swings. Has to do with help from the Lord. Has to do with being who you are, mentally, spiritually, and in terms of self-understanding. Has to do with not being weighed down with guilt feelings. Has to do with feeling normal about myself.

It's an error to think that all mental illness stimuli are self-generated. It also reflects an ignorance of spiritual realities and powers which the scriptures clearly portray. It also doesn't reflect insight into the actual subjective realities which mentally ill persons experience of themselves and his world.

Many times this perspective reflects the bias of modern science, which views life and experience in a purely mechanical and instrumental way. It assumes all stimuli can be brought under control and into submission simply by orchestrating the brain's chemistry, or by affecting chemical imbalances in such a way as to bring balance and healing to the mind.

I'm not disputing the positive effects of medicine. I'm just trying to suggest there are spiritual realities to mental illness as well.

The successful research and the dedication of mental health professionals are extremely important in the process of bringing health to the mentally ill also.

The problem is not so much to classify and objectify the features of mental illness. The problem is to deal with these stimuli successfully. The issue is partly a matter of psychological integration as well. The symptoms of a mentally ill person often change over time. With the help of medication they can be managed more successfully over time. Periodic problems which come up can be managed and there can be psychological and spiritual healing.

So pray for the doctor, pray for the nurse. Try to be responsive to them and the work they are trying to do on your behalf. Give of your time and energy to help them do the work which they are called to do. Give of yourself so that they may understand you and aid you as you seek to live a good, happy life without the terror and pain of serious illness.

His house

I'm more content to simply dwell in my own abode. My house has been cool and comfortable all summer, which has been really nice. We've had great weather.

Is my house O.K.—need some repairs? How's my yard—it is looking real good, I might say. I have beautiful grounds, and a very nice, very comfortable old house. I like my situation very much.

My house is quite a wonderful haven, a beacon in the night. My feelings for my house have been developing for some time. It seems very accommodating, very livable for me. I think Eureka likes the house well too. Together we inhabit this space; these walls, doors and ceilings. Thank you, Lord, for a happy situation, for an absence of violence and hatred in the neighborhood.

Humbleness

There just doesn't seem to be anything great or grand about what I do. It seems I leave that for others. I have no honors, or social standing, or much recognition for who I am and what I do. The people I share my good with are others of my humanity and treat me well but not with any preferential or deferential treatment. Still it is a life. A good life in a real sense. I feel good. I'm active and creative, and I have a lot of very rewarding relationships.

Who knows, maybe I'm the smallest piece of material in the universe. People seem to run over me pretty well, pretty easily. I'm not much of a challenge or a problem for anyone. I keep to myself pretty well. At any rate whatever I am or may be is only a minor hint of what I am and will be.

Death

I'll probably die all alone. I don't know when now. It probably won't be for a long time. Death doesn't really sound too interesting to me right now. It might more later. I don't really know. Someone doesn't like to die too much right now. In fact, fights it vociferously, tooth and nail. It's part of life though, isn't it?

Someday there will come an end to everything, and then a new life will come, with God and man. That's not really death though. That's life—eternal life.

I feel like I can die in peace because my eyes have seen the salvation of the Lord. He is good. He is the good shepherd, who cares for the sheep. He gives rest to the weary, strength to the faint. There is nothing he cannot do.

I don't really know what death is like for a Christian, but I believe I will be with the Lord in some really substantial way.

His conversion and recommitment

Shortly before going to college I had a dramatic conversion experience. I was convinced that Christianity was the right way for everyone and that I had found the source of real life. I knew that I had to go to college. It seemed like quite a challenge to integrate what I had learned with the classroom.

I arrived in Ann Arbor, the University of Michigan, in early September of 1972. It was like entering into the lion's den. I had signed up in a dormitory, which was the center of all kinds of activity that I no longer considered helpful. It was hard to share my faith with others. I did make some friends. I began to meet with a Christian support group composed of members of a charismatic community and received some support there. I was suffering a great deal with feelings of alienation and rejection, and these men helped me feel more at home.

I have just finished rededicating my life to Jesus as my Savior and Lord. I want to live my life in his presence. I acknowledge that he has the power to save me and the grace to sustain me in that conviction. I want to go forward in this new way with more confidence and hope for the future. He is my Lord and Savior.

I realize this will be a battle. I am having problems with not liking myself and I know the difficulty is pretty deep-seated. Self-hatred, along with sexual tensions and homicidal thoughts, tends to bring me down to a point where I lose heart. I must pray daily for the courage to fight and win.

If I can get my Christian life going better, I believe I can gain confidence that my life can be worthwhile and fruitful.

The Lord

The Lord helps me to take a stand. I can manage standing in the kitchen today!

The Lord is our doctor, our shepherd. He is equal to the task. The Lord is strong. The Lord is mighty, the Lord is great. The Lord will see me through to the end, to the coming day. The Lord preserves the lives of those who trust in him.

The Lord has given me a good Monday. I'd say he is beyond belief, but that probably wouldn't be saying too much. Really I just want to say I am in awe of what he has done in my life. He truly is the Lord and

God. He has authored my life, he has protected me, he has allowed me to share in his grace. All the hoopla about other things in life is just that. The Lord is the one who really matters, who is the giver of all good gifts.

I run to the shelter of the cross.

While God's grace is free and unmerited, it came at a cost, the price of the life of Jesus Christ. Christ died, so that we might live. There is an irony here, a paradox, that the just should die for the unjust. That the righteous should die for the unrighteous. That the godly should die for the ungodly, that God should die for man. But it is clear that it is the only possible way in which salvation could come to us, and to the whole world. Someone had to pay the price for sin, and Jesus the Son of God, the Lord of glory, did. He suffered in the body on the cross. He took the curse of death upon himself, which had hung on creation since the fall. He broke the power of sin and death, suffering, by rising on the third day in accordance with the Scripture. He redeemed our bodies by his act of redemption. He opened a path into heaven, breaking the hold of death and Hades. He will someday return in glory, for his own. He will make us fully like him then, changing our lowly bodies to be like his glorious body on that day.

You are never alone with Jesus Christ in your life. He is the ultimate person, the best friend one can have. He is the ultimate source of security, of love and peace. He is so great and so strong, He is always able to help you, and what's more, he doesn't mind doing it. He is such a wonderful, wonderful Savior. To know you won't ever have to be alone, with Jesus Christ there, is perhaps the most profound of life's blessings. I have experienced a lot of closeness, and the mercy of Christ's ongoing presence and ministry.

My life has been blessed by the Lord. He gives strength. He gives rest. He saves. He leads. He helps. I've sometimes felt funny about asking for the Lord's help. Certainly someone else might need it more. What have I done to deserve his favor? Nothing. But that's not why he helps us. He helps us out of his great storehouse of grace. He is generous.

He is kind. He is faithful to his word. "No one who trusts in him will be put to shame." That includes me. I can trust and hope in his word.

I get so frightened and rattled at times. What would I do if I didn't have Jesus to turn to. I don't know. I don't think I could make it through life without him. He is faithful.

Through my personal roller coaster, the thing that seems to remain most constant is the grace of God in Christ.

Can you imagine life without Jesus Christ? Not really. He is the life that is life indeed. He is the living water for all who thirst. He is the bread of life for all who hunger. He is the treasure of all the world's true poor. He is my life indeed.

The Lord leads us from one degree of glory to the next. He is perfect, sure, and able. He is able to save, able to give all good things to us. Those who love and follow him will never be disappointed. He is the dawn treader, the harbinger of things to come; the waking of the new day, the ever-present principle of new life, welling up to eternity. It is the Lord who is to be glorified, not man and his accomplishments. The Lord and his word will abide forever. "Turn back oh foolish man!"

I find the meaning for my life, in his, in his life and death. He is my heart's desire. He is my joy and my song. He is my Lord too. I belong to him, body and soul. He is my creator, my maker. He truly is very God of very God. My Savior, my God, and my King. Oh, to be in his presence, always.

Christmas poem

written November, 2003, shortly before Dave died:

God's Gift to Us

Give as if all the giving was done,
Give as we receive life from the Son.
Give out of the generosity of your heart,
Give in word, deed, and art.

Give to the ones you love,
Like God's gift from above.
Give because it is Jesus Christ's day,
Give to him in every way.

The Lord is coming again,
Every heart prepare him room.
Let everything that has breath praise the Lord.
And let us all thank him in one accord.

Give thanks to God, his way is true,
And know that he is watching over you.

Final Reflections on Telling This Story of Billy and Dave

Going over in our minds the history of these two sons has reawakened in us a host of feelings. It has put us in touch again with the extent of their sufferings (Billy seemed largely unaware of his; Dave's were always painfully felt). It has reminded us again of how often we were totally at a loss, broken-hearted, near despair. We feel afresh some of the bitter disappointments we knew, the doubts and fears that plagued us. It recalled to us our desperate searchings for light and our anguished cries to God. It brought back memories of long years in which everything else seemed to be played out in an atmosphere of sadness and anxiety. Plaintive, mournful was the background music of those days.

When all of that comes rushing back, we ask ourselves, "Why do we want to tell this story? Why reawaken old griefs? Why share what was so acutely painful? Who needs to hear about our brokenness, our shattered dreams?"

Our answer is that the brokenness is only part of the story. There's also the *blessing.* What thrills us, what cheers our hearts, is to think of the people Billy and Dave became in their latter years. We always smile when we think of Billy's joy in small things (he would clap his weakened right hand almost raw when a White Sox pitcher even threw a strike!), of the pleasure and fun he gave to all the family, of his wild glee in riding on a golf cart through a rainstorm, of his cheerfulness in situations that got the rest of us down. It moves us to think of how marvelously happy he was in spite of all his limitations. And though his Christian faith was never very informed or reasoned, his trust in Jesus was serene. He lived in the moment, anxiety-free. Isn't that a lot to celebrate!

And then there's Dave. We are awed and overjoyed at the man he became in the closing chapters of his life. We've already touched on his extraordinary gratefulness for everything he received. We've celebrated his gift of encouraging others in their struggles, his persistent caring for people in need. Dave was a prince among wounded healers. He took great delight in all his family members, valuing their successes almost more than his own. Out of meager means, he was generous to a fault.

What we remember especially as parents was his remarkable warmth toward us. He was always affirming us lavishly—the one person in the world who stoutly believed that his dad should be president of the US! He was tender in concern for our well-being, asking us daily how we were doing. He would call his dad early in the morning to read him a journal entry just written. He would call his mom day after day to say how much he loved her. We wonder, did any parents ever have a more affirming son?

"But," someone asks, "doesn't all that make the pain of losing them that much greater?" We answer, "Yes!" It surely does. How we miss them! How our whole family feels diminished and deprived because they're not with us! But the parting is also a "sweet sorrow" because of rich memories that linger like a fragrance.

"But the dying of each of them was so sudden! What a shock that must have been for you and your family!" Indeed it was. Yet, as time passes, we see a mercy even in that. Both sons were in declining health when they died. Billy was growing weaker through a hip fracture and reduced lung capacity, perhaps soon to be bed-ridden. Dave was struggling with heart disease and high blood sugar, retaining fluid, headed perhaps toward debilitating illness. Both died supremely happy—Billy after his best vacation ever; Dave after watching a great half of Hope basketball. And both, by God's grace, have departed to be "with Christ," which, the apostle Paul assures us "is far better."

Finally, we want to bear grateful witness to what all this has meant to us as a family. We're told that marriages with handicapped children are more likely than most to break up. The statistics for families who experience mental illness are even more grim. We must have been in double jeopardy. But it has not been so in our marriage. The strains upon family bonds through our trials have been enormous, and we have sometimes been at odds. Hard words have been spoken. But somehow the shared suffering has knit us together tightly. Both of us sense that our love for each other is warmer and deeper than ever.

Words can't describe fully how much our two living sons, Jim and Jonathan, with their wives Kathy and Jeannette, have meant to us in our sorrows. They are a comfort to us beyond measure. They care for us and support us in a thousand practical ways. They treasure what matters most to us, and serve the Lord whole-heartedly. They also seem seasoned by sorrow, their love deepened and made tender, their faith refined as by fire. They, together with our six grandchildren, each filled with promise, are the great gladness of our latter years.

We owe huge thanks also to the dear friends who have stood by us in our trials. They have been there when we most needed them, easing our sorrows with their help and comfort, doubling our joys by sharing them. They have many times been the very presence of Jesus to our lives. Bless them!

So, with all of this in our hearts, we tell our story: from brokenness to blessedness. All kinds of things have contributed to our brokenness, but the blessing has a single source. It's the Lord. It's the God of our salvation, Father, Son, and Holy Spirit. He's the One who gives "beauty for ashes, the oil of joy for mourning, and the garment of praise for the spirit of heaviness." To God we give glory, praise, and thanks. We are filled with awe and wonder at the grace we see in the life, death, and rising of Jesus. We rejoice that nothing can ever separate us from God's love in Christ. We testify with joy that "behind a frowning providence, he hides a smiling face." All praise to the One who, out of brokenness, often gives his choicest blessing!

—Bill and Helen

About the Brownsons

Bill Brownson is a graduate of Davidson College in North Carolina and of Columbia Seminary in Decatur, Georgia. He holds a doctorate in New Testament studies from Princeton Theological Seminary. He has served as pastor of Reformed churches in New Jersey and Chicago, as professor of preaching at Western Theological Seminary, and as President and Broadcast Minister for Words of Hope, an international radio outreach of the Reformed Church in America.

• • •

Helen Brownson graduated from Wheaton College in Illinois, and received a Master's degree from Western Michigan University. For many years, she administered special needs programs for the Holland Public Schools. She also served foster care facilities for two years, and following that became the Minister of Outreach at Christ Memorial Reformed Church in Holland, Michigan.

• • •

Jim Brownson graduated from the University of Michigan and from Western Theological Seminary. He holds a doctorate in New Testament studies from Princeton Theological Seminary. He has served as pastor of a Reformed congregation in Traverse City, Michigan, as an instructor at Calvin College in Grand Rapids, Michigan, and as academic dean at Western Seminary. He is presently the James and Jean Cook Professor of New Testament at Western Seminary.

• • •

Jonathan Brownson graduated from the University of Michigan and from Western Theological Seminary. He received a Master's degree from Lutheran School of Theology in Chicago and a Doctor of Ministry degree from Western Seminary. He has served as pastor of congregations in Illinois, Georgia, and Michigan. He presently serves the Reformed Church in America as its first Minister of Prayer.